The New fondue Cookbook

From Savory Ale-Spiked Cheddar Fondue to Sweet Chocolate Peanut Butter Fondue, 100 Recipes for Fondue Fun!

Adams Media

New York   London   Toronto   Sydney   New Delhi

Adams Media
An Imprint of Simon & Schuster, Inc.
57 Littlefield Street
Avon, Massachusetts 02322

First Adams Media hardcover edition December 2020

ADAMS MEDIA and colophon are trademarks of Simon & Schuster.

For information about special discounts for bulk purchases, please contact Simon & Schuster Special Sales at 1-866-506-1949 or business@simonandschuster.com.

The Simon & Schuster Speakers Bureau can bring authors to your live event. For more information or to book an event contact the Simon & Schuster Speakers Bureau at 1-866-248-3049 or visit our website at www.simonspeakers.com.

Interior design by Julia Jacintho
Photographs by Harper Point Photography

Manufactured in the United States of America

10 9 8 7 6 5 4 3 2 1

Library of Congress Cataloging-in-Publication Data
Authors: Adams Media (firm).
Title: The new fondue cookbook.
Description: First Adams Media hardcover edition. | Avon, Massachusetts: Adams Media, 2020. | Includes index.
Identifiers: LCCN 2020034562 | ISBN 9781507214459 (hc) | ISBN 9781507214466 (ebook)
Subjects: LCSH: Fondue. | LCGFT: Cookbooks.
Classification: LCC TX825 .N49 2020 | DDC 641.81--dc23
LC record available at https://lccn.loc.gov/2020034562

ISBN 978-1-5072-1445-9
ISBN 978-1-5072-1446-6 (ebook)

Contains material adapted from the following titles published by Adams Media, an Imprint of Simon & Schuster, Inc.: *The Everything® Fondue Cookbook* by Rhonda Lauret Parkinson, copyright © 2004, ISBN 978-1-59337-119-7 and *The Everything® Fondue Party Book* by Belinda Hulin, copyright © 2006, ISBN 978-1-59337-702-1.

Contents

Part Two

SWEET FONDUES...85

Introduction

Ale-Spiked Cheddar Fondue

Bourbon and Butterscotch Fondue

S'mores Fondue

You may think fondue is just bubbling pots of delicious cheese or chocolate—and it can be—but it's also so much more!

Fondues can be hot or cold, sweet or savory, appetizers, desserts, or main dishes. You could make a three-course meal entirely out of fondue! Soups, curries, egg rolls, drinks, and even breakfast foods—the list of what you can turn into a fondue is only limited by your imagination! Fondue is all about experimentation, and *The New Fondue Cookbook* is here to help you plan the perfect fondue for any occasion. Here you'll find one hundred delicious recipes, including:

- Savory Scallop and Sake Fondue
- Cajun Hot Pepper Cheese Fondue
- Champagne Fondue
- Raspberry Swirl Fondue
- Pumpkin Cheesecake Fondue
- Chocolate Cherry Cordial Fondue

Fondue takes very little preparation, the ingredients are affordable, and you don't have to spend hours in the kitchen stressing about it! Not only that, but also everyone can cook the food according to his or her own preference. And let's not forget that it's just plain fun to skewer your own food and dip it!

The important thing to remember is this: A fondue is a way to bring people together to share a meal. So don't be afraid to experiment! All the classic fondue dishes started with ingredients on hand and a creative cook—so feel free to start your own fondue traditions. This book will both inspire your dinners and delight your senses, so warm up your fondue pot and let's get melting!

Fon-Dos and Fon-Don'ts: Health and Safety

While you don't need to have a party to have some fondue, fondue is by nature a communal experience. No matter how exclusive your guest list, or how pricey your ingredients, a fondue meal has a casual air. Still, there are a few rules to ensure everybody's safety and comfort:

- Never fill a pot more than ⅓ full for oil fondue. If oil must be reheated or more oil added, move the fondue pot away from the heat source and away from your guests. Handle refreshing the oil in the kitchen, then carefully return the pot to the table.
- Never refuel an alcohol-fueled pot while it's still hot. The burner attachment must be completely cool before fuel is added.
- Always carefully read the instructions that come with your fondue set. Different heat sources have slightly different requirements and procedures.
- Have enough plates, skewers, forks, and dipping bowls on hand to discourage your guests from redipping already nibbled items into the fondue pot or sauce bowls.
- Keep raw meats and seafood away from breads, vegetables, and other ready-to-eat items. Meats and seafood should be prepared, then either served immediately or covered and refrigerated until ready to serve.
- Have antibacterial wipes ready to mop up spills or dropped ingredients.
- Raw eggs carry a risk of salmonella. Some Asian hot pots call for a dipping sauce of raw egg. You may want to consider using pasteurized eggs or skipping raw egg sauces altogether.
- Oil and broth fondue mixtures must stay hot enough to cook meats and shellfish thoroughly.

Finally, to avoid the problem of double-dipping, put a large basket of skewers next to the fondue pot. Put regular forks at everyone's place, or a basket of regular or disposable forks next to buffet plates. Your guests will quickly get the idea—dunk with the skewers, move the food onto a plate, and eat with the regular fork. In the case of vegetables, fruits, or long chunks of bread, guests can just dip one end into the pot, much as they might help themselves to chips and salsa. Remember these simple health and safety tips, and have fun fondue-ing!

Part One
SAVORY FONDUES

Appenzeller Cider Fondue

Serves 6

If your party includes nondrinkers or kids, use regular apple cider or apple juice in place of hard cider. If you want the flavor of alcohol without the kick, use a mixture of half apple juice, half alcohol-free white wine.

Ingredients

1½ cups dry hard cider

1 pound Appenzeller cheese, shredded

½ pound Emmentaler cheese, shredded

⅛ teaspoon ground nutmeg

¼ teaspoon white pepper

2 teaspoons cornstarch

1 tablespoon kirsch

3 cups toasted and diced challah bread

3 cups toasted and diced sunflower seed bread

1. In a medium saucepan over medium heat, bring cider to a simmer. Add shredded cheeses in four batches, stirring in a figure-eight motion until each batch is melted.

2. Add nutmeg and pepper and stir to combine.

3. In a small bowl, dissolve cornstarch in kirsch. Heat fondue until bubbly and stir in cornstarch mixture. Reduce heat and simmer 2 minutes.

4. Pour mixture into a fondue pot and keep warm over low heat.

5. Serve fondue with challah and sunflower seed bread.

A Cheesy Twist

If you want a more exotic (cheese-speaking) flavor in your fondue, try substituting the Emmentaler in this recipe with some Vacherin Fribourgeois. Vacherin Fribourgeois is a semi-soft, slightly acidic cow's milk cheese with a high fat content. Remove the dull yellow rind before melting.

French Brie Fondue

Serves 6

Everything tastes better with Brie! This fondue is so versatile, so don't hold yourself back with just the traditional bread cubes or baguette dippers. Try pretzels, popcorn, fresh fruit, or dried fruit like dried apricots, papaya, and pineapple.

Ingredients

3 tablespoons butter

3 tablespoons all-purpose flour

1½ cups half and half

16 ounces Brie, rind removed

1 clove garlic, peeled

½ cup parsley

2 medium green onions, trimmed and cut in thirds

2 tablespoons fresh tarragon

⅛ teaspoon black pepper

1. In a medium saucepan over medium heat, melt butter. Add flour and stir until blended.

2. Slowly whisk in half and half. Cook until mixture is smooth and slightly thickened.

3. Dice Brie and stir into mixture, using a figure-eight motion. Stir frequently until cheese is completely melted.

4. Place garlic, parsley, green onions, and tarragon leaves in a food processor. Process until herbs are all finely minced. Stir into cheese mixture. Add pepper.

5. Raise heat to medium-high and cook until bubbly. Pour into fondue pot, place over heat source set to low, and serve.

> ### Brie Alternatives
> *For variety, you can use a mixture of Brie with Camembert and other soft cheeses. For a less expensive dish, use 8 ounces of full-fat cream cheese with 4 ounces of blue cheese in place of the Brie. Although these are all high-moisture cheeses, the roux in the recipe helps produce a good, thick fondue.*

Emmentaler Cheese Fondue

Serves 8

Time for a cheese lesson! Emmentaler is the original hole-filled Swiss cheese, and while it looks like your standard Swiss cheese, it's not. Emmentaler is a bit sweeter and milder than regular Swiss cheese. For this dish, you'll want to splurge on authentic Emmentaler rather than a generic Swiss cheese.

Ingredients

2 cups sauvignon blanc

2 cloves garlic, peeled and pressed

Juice of 2 medium lemons

1 pound Gruyère cheese

1 pound Emmentaler cheese

1½ tablespoons cornstarch

3 tablespoons kirsch

½ teaspoon white pepper

¼ cup minced parsley

½ teaspoon ground nutmeg

Cubed bread, including French, rye, wheat, and pumpernickel

1. In a medium heavy saucepan over medium heat, pour in wine. Add pressed garlic to pan along with lemon juice. Bring mixture to a simmer.

2. Shred cheeses in a food processor. Add ¼ cheese to the simmering liquid and stir in a figure-eight pattern. Once that cheese has melted, add another ¼ cheese to the saucepan. Keep stirring. Repeat until all cheese is melted and mixture is hot but not boiling.

3. In a small bowl, dissolve cornstarch in kirsch. Stir into cheese mixture. Cook until just bubbly, then reduce heat and simmer 1 minute.

4. Add pepper, parsley, and nutmeg to melted cheese and stir well.

5. Pour liquid into fondue pot and keep warm over heat source on low heat. Serve with assorted bread cubes for dipping.

Gorgonzola Fondue

Serves 12

Gorgonzola adds a rich, nutty flavor to dishes that some people may find a bit too strong. Fortunately, in this recipe, the cream and cream cheese give the Gorgonzola a milder edge. Serve this fondue with crusty sourdough bread and vegetables.

Ingredients

2 cups heavy cream

1 pound Gorgonzola cheese, crumbled

1 pound cream cheese

1 medium shallot, minced

1 clove garlic, peeled and minced

1 tablespoon cornstarch

2 tablespoons whole milk

⅛ teaspoon black pepper

1. In a large saucepan over medium heat, warm cream until hot but not boiling. Add Gorgonzola crumbles by the handful, stirring in a figure-eight motion until each addition is melted.

2. Add cream cheese, 1 tablespoonful at a time, stirring well after each addition.

3. Add shallot and garlic, then increase heat slightly.

4. In a small bowl, combine cornstarch and milk, stirring until smooth. When cheese mixture begins to bubble, add cornstarch mixture to it. Reduce heat and simmer, stirring, until mixture is thick and smooth. Stir in black pepper.

5. Ladle hot mixture into a fondue pot and place over heat source set to low. Serve.

> **Shopping Adventures**
>
> *Farmers' markets and supermarkets offer a treasure trove of unusual produce. Make your table a conversation starter with multi-colored, bite-sized sweet peppers, purple fingerling potatoes, and orange cauliflower—all perfect for dipping in this fondue!*

Three Cheese Fondue

Serves 6

It's true that Tilsit is a stinky cheese, but don't be put off by its, shall we say, pungent odor. This Danish cheese has an intriguing spicy taste that makes a nice complement to the Gruyère in this fondue.

Ingredients

1 clove garlic, smashed, peeled, and cut in half

1½ cups dry white wine

1 tablespoon lemon juice

½ pound Gruyère cheese, finely diced

½ pound Emmentaler cheese, finely diced

½ pound Tilsit cheese, finely diced

1 teaspoon cornstarch

2 tablespoons kirsch

⅛ teaspoon white pepper

1 sprig parsley, chopped

1 medium loaf stale bread, toasted and cut into cubes

1. Rub garlic around the inside of a medium saucepan. Discard garlic. Add wine to the pan and warm over medium-low heat. Don't allow wine to boil.

2. When wine is warm, stir in lemon juice. Add cheeses, a handful at a time. Stir cheese continually in a sideways figure-eight pattern. Wait until cheese is completely melted before adding more. Don't allow the fondue mixture to boil.

3. When cheese is completely melted, dissolve cornstarch in kirsch in a small bowl and then stir into the fondue. Turn up the heat until it is just bubbling and starting to thicken. Stir in white pepper and parsley.

4. Transfer to a fondue pot and set over the heat source on low heat. Serve with bread cubes for dipping.

> ### Thickening a Cheese Fondue
> *Having trouble getting the fondue to thicken? Turn up the heat, add a bit of cornstarch mixed with water, and stir quickly with a whisk. Another option is simply to add more cheese.*

Spiced Feta-Spinach Fondue

Serves 12

The classic combination of spinach and feta gets a new life in this pot of cheesy fondue goodness. Authentic feta is made from sheep's milk, although many supermarket versions are made from cow's milk. Either type will work here. Try this fondue with bread, vegetables, and cooked lamb cubes.

Ingredients

2 cups whole milk

1 pound feta cheese, crumbled

1 pound whole milk ricotta cheese

2 cloves garlic, peeled and pressed

1 pound fresh spinach, cooked

½ cup parsley

2 medium green onions, chopped

1 tablespoon cornstarch

2 tablespoons water

¼ teaspoon ground nutmeg

¼ teaspoon ground cinnamon

⅛ teaspoon black pepper

1. In a large saucepan over medium heat, heat milk until just scalded. Add feta and ricotta cheese to hot milk in batches, stirring in a figure-eight motion until cheese is melted and mixture is smooth. Add pressed garlic.

2. Press excess moisture from spinach. Place in a food processor with parsley and green onions. Pulse until chopped, but not puréed.

3. In a small bowl, combine cornstarch and water. Stir until smooth and then add to cheese mixture. Heat until cheese is bubbly. Add spinach mixture and stir well.

4. Add nutmeg, cinnamon, and pepper.

5. Ladle into a fondue pot and place pot over heat source set to low. Serve.

> ### Bread Basics
> *Always serve hearty breads that can stand up to dunking. For variety, try tossing bread cubes in olive oil, sprinkle with sea salt or herbs, and bake in a single layer at 350°F until crisp.*

Garlicky Vaud Fondue

Serves 6

Even if you can't get to the beautiful slopes of Vaud in Switzerland, this hearty, casual fondue is perfect for cool-weather entertaining. Stoke the fireplace and invite friends to drop in for board games and a cozy treat! Serve this fondue with 1" baguette rounds and mixed sausages.

Ingredients

1 small head garlic

1 tablespoon olive oil

1½ cups dry white wine

Juice of 2 medium lemons

1 pound Gruyère cheese, shredded

½ pound Emmentaler cheese, shredded

½ teaspoon black pepper

2 teaspoons cornstarch

1 tablespoon brandy

1. Preheat oven to 350°F.

2. Remove outer skin from garlic head, leaving head intact. Rub garlic with olive oil and wrap in heavy foil. Bake for 1 hour. Set aside until cool enough to handle. Pull cloves apart and squeeze garlic from cloves into a dish.

3. In a medium saucepan over medium heat, heat wine and lemon juice until hot but not boiling.

4. Add cheeses to liquid in four batches, stirring in a figure-eight motion, until each addition is melted. Add roasted garlic to cheese and mix until well blended. Sprinkle in black pepper. Heat fondue until bubbly.

5. In a small bowl, dissolve cornstarch in brandy and then stir into fondue. Simmer 2 minutes, then pour fondue into fondue pot and place over the heat source set to low. Serve.

Northern Italian Fonduta

Serves 6

This recipe is an ultra-rich fondue based on a classic dish from the mountains of north-west Italy. Don't cheap out and buy sliced, packaged Fontina: It won't taste the same. Go for the real thing for this dish. If you'd like you can sprinkle a little grated Asiago cheese into the mix to deepen the flavor.

Ingredients

6 tablespoons butter

2 tablespoons all-purpose flour

2 cups heavy cream

4 medium egg yolks

1½ pounds Fontina cheese, finely chopped or shredded

½ teaspoon white truffle oil

⅛ teaspoon white pepper

1. In a large saucepan over medium heat, melt butter. Sprinkle in flour and stir with a wooden spoon until roux is smooth and bubbly. Slowly add cream and cook, stirring until mixture is hot and thickened.

2. In a large bowl, whisk egg yolks together. While whisking, slowly pour a ladle of hot cream into eggs. When it's blended, quickly whisk it into the saucepan.

3. Working in batches, stir Fontina into cream mixture using a figure-eight motion. Wait until one batch has completely melted before adding the next. When mixture is completely melted and bubbly, add white truffle oil and pepper.

4. Remove from heat. Pour fonduta into fondue pot and set over heat source on low heat.

Cajun Hot Pepper Cheese Fondue

Serves 12

Beer, cheese, and spice—it's a trifecta of deliciousness. This fondue isn't for the faint of heart—or stomach. Make sure there's plenty of bread available. Serve this fondue with crusty bread, tortilla chips, sausages, and vegetables for dipping.

Ingredients

2 cups beer

1 pound smoked Gouda cheese, shredded

8 ounces white Cheddar cheese, crumbled

8 ounces Gruyère cheese, shredded

2 cloves garlic, peeled and pressed

1 medium yellow onion, peeled and finely chopped

½ cup finely chopped green onion

½ cup finely chopped parsley

1 small red bell pepper, seeded and finely diced

1 tablespoon cornstarch

2 tablespoons water

2 tablespoons Tabasco sauce

1. In a large saucepan over medium heat, warm the beer. Add cheeses in four batches, stirring in a figure-eight motion until each batch is completely melted.

2. Add garlic, onions, parsley, and bell pepper to the mixture. Heat until bubbly.

3. In a small bowl, combine cornstarch and water. Stir until smooth. Add to cheese mixture.

4. Continue cooking and stirring 1–2 minutes. Add Tabasco. Stir.

5. Remove cheese mixture to a fondue pot. Place over the heat source set to low heat and serve.

Sherry-Poached Chicken and Veal Fondue

Serves 8

How much sherry you'll need for this fondue depends largely on the size and depth of your fondue pots. Count on at least 3 cups per fondue pot. Serve this fondue with dipping sauces of your choice.

Ingredients

4 (4-ounce) boneless, skinless chicken breasts

8 (3-ounce) veal cutlets, pounded thin

3 tablespoons olive oil

⅛ teaspoon salt

⅛ teaspoon black pepper

2 cups fresh spinach leaves, stems removed

½ cup parsley

6 cloves garlic, peeled

Manzanilla dry sherry

1. With a sharp knife, reduce the thickness of chicken breasts by slicing each piece in half vertically. With a stone or nonstick rolling pin, flatten each chicken slice into thin cutlets.

2. Coat top side of each chicken and veal cutlet with olive oil and sprinkle salt and pepper.

3. In a food processor, finely chop spinach, parsley, and garlic. Sprinkle a thin layer of spinach mixture over the top of each cutlet.

4. Working from the longest side, roll cutlets tightly into a pinwheel. Secure each pinwheel with a toothpick. Slice each pinwheel horizontally into 1" slices. Place alternating veal and chicken pinwheels on fondue skewers.

5. In a small saucepan over medium heat, heat sherry on the stovetop until bubbles just start to appear around the edges. Pour hot sherry into one or more fondue pots. You should have enough to reach halfway up the edge of the pot. Guests can place skewers in simmering sherry until chicken and veal are thoroughly cooked.

Marinated Chicken Wings

Serves 6

The lemon-garlic chicken wings are easy and delicious. Serve them alongside some rice and a salad for a complete meal or as an appetizer at your next big-game party.

Mediterranean Chicken Marinade Ingredients

2 cloves garlic, smashed and peeled

½ cup olive oil

2 tablespoons plus 1 teaspoon lemon juice

1½ teaspoons fresh tarragon leaves

Fondue Ingredients

2 pounds chicken wings

5 cups vegetable oil, or as needed

1. In a medium bowl, combine marinade ingredients. Set aside.

2. **For chicken:** Rinse chicken wings and pat dry. Cut through wings at the joints.

3. Place wings in a shallow glass dish and brush with the marinade on both sides. Refrigerate chicken and allow to marinate 1 hour. Pat dry and remove any excess marinade.

4. **For fondue:** Add oil to the fondue pot, making sure it is not more than half full. Heat the pot on a stove element over medium-high heat.

5. When oil is hot, move the fondue pot to the table and set over the heat source at low heat. Use dipping forks or metal skewers to skewer chicken wings. Cook in the hot oil until wings are browned and cooked through.

> ### *Marinating Times*
> *Beef and chicken should be marinated for 1 hour. By contrast, it takes only 15–30 minutes for the marinade to penetrate most types of seafood. Take care not to marinate too long, or the meat or fish may turn soft and mushy.*

Ale-Spiked Cheddar Fondue

Serves 12

This fondue is perfect for your next tailgate party. The fondue can be made at home, transported in a heat-safe dish to a tailgate site, then warmed up in a fondue pot. You can use nonalcoholic beer in place of the ale when serving a crowd that includes non-drinkers. Serve this fondue with hearty breads and pretzels for dipping. Go Team!

Ingredients

2 cups ale

1 pound sharp Cheddar cheese, shredded

1 pound medium Cheddar cheese, shredded

1 small yellow onion, peeled and finely chopped

1 teaspoon Worcestershire sauce

1½ tablespoons cornstarch

2 tablespoons whole milk

⅛ teaspoon cayenne pepper

1. In a large saucepan over medium heat, heat ale until simmering. Add cheese in four batches, stirring in a figure-eight motion until each batch is melted.

2. Stir in onion and Worcestershire sauce. Increase heat to medium-high heat.

3. In a small bowl, dissolve cornstarch in milk and then add to cheese mixture. Cook until smooth, thick, and bubbly. Add cayenne pepper.

4. Pour into fondue pot and place over heat source set to low. Serve.

> **Getting Cheesy**
> *A bold Cheddar fondue will add just the right amount of variety to your tailgate menu. For the main course, stick with something substantial and familiar. We suggest sausages, but grilled burgers, steaks, or chops would work as well.*

Parmigiano-Reggiano Classic Fondue

Serves 6

This hot bubbling pot of cheese, wine, and ham is sure to be a hit at your next fondue party.

Ingredients

1 tablespoon all-purpose flour

1 tablespoon dried oregano

4 ounces Parmigiano-Reggiano cheese, finely diced

6 ounces Gorgonzola cheese, finely diced

4 ounces Asiago cheese

1 clove garlic, peeled and cut in half

1 cup dry white wine

1 tablespoon lemon juice

2 tablespoons chopped cooked ham

1 fresh truffle, thinly sliced

Basic Bruschetta (see sidebar), cut into cubes

1. In a medium bowl, mix flour with oregano. Toss Parmigiano-Reggiano and Gorgonzola cheeses with the seasoned flour. Crumble Asiago cheese into the mixture.

2. Rub garlic around the inside of a medium saucepan. Discard garlic. Add wine to the saucepan and warm over medium-low heat. Don't allow wine to boil.

3. When wine is warm, stir in lemon juice. Add cheese, a handful at a time. Stir cheese continually in a sideways figure-eight pattern. Wait until cheese is completely melted before adding more.

4. When cheese is melted, turn up the heat until it is just bubbling and starting to thicken. Transfer to a fondue pot and set over the heat source on low heat. Just before serving, sprinkle with chopped ham and sliced truffle. Serve with bruschetta cubes for dipping.

> ### Basic Bruschetta
> *You'll need 1 medium baguette, 2 smashed cloves garlic that are peeled and cut in half, and ½ cup extra-virgin olive oil. To make, cut baguette into ½" slices. Turn the oven to broil. Broil baguette in the oven on both sides. Rub garlic over both sides of the toasted baguette slices. Brush with olive oil. Your bruschetta is now ready to serve.*

Italian Pesto Fondue with Cheese

Serves 6

Pesto breathes new life into a traditional Fontina cheese fondue. The nutty, cheesy Fontina is amplified by the briny, salty pesto to create a fresh and bright dish that is sure to become a fan favorite. Serve this with soft breadsticks for dipping.

Ingredients

1 tablespoon cornstarch

½ teaspoon dried oregano

¼ pound Fontina cheese, finely diced

½ pound Gruyère cheese, finely diced

1 clove garlic, peeled and cut in half

1 cup dry white wine

2 teaspoons lemon juice

½ cup jarred pesto

1. In a medium bowl, mix cornstarch with oregano. Toss diced cheeses with cornstarch mixture.

2. Rub garlic around the inside of a medium saucepan. Discard garlic. Add wine to the saucepan and warm over medium-low heat. Don't allow wine to boil. Remove ¼ cup wine and keep warm over low heat in a separate small saucepan.

3. When wine is warm in the medium saucepan, stir in lemon juice. Add cheese, a handful at a time. Stir cheese continually in a sideways figure-eight pattern. Wait until cheese is completely melted before adding more. Don't allow the fondue mixture to boil.

4. When cheese is melted, turn up the heat until it is just bubbling and starting to thicken. Stir in pesto. Add remaining ¼ cup wine if necessary for consistency.

5. Transfer to a fondue pot and set over the heat source on low heat. Serve.

Curry Fondue

Serves 4

No need to run out to an Indian restaurant to get your curry craving satisfied. This fondue has all the warming flavors of curry in a creamy, cheesy package—and without having to leave your house!

Ingredients

2 medium green jalapeño peppers

1 clove garlic, smashed and peeled

1¼ cups white wine

2 teaspoons lemon juice

¼ pound aged Cheddar cheese, diced

¼ pound Havarti cheese with dill, diced

½ pound Gruyère cheese, finely diced

1 tablespoon cornstarch

1½ tablespoons kirsch

1¼ teaspoons mild curry powder

Basic Bruschetta (see Parmigiano-Reggiano Classic Fondue recipe in this part), cut into cubes

12–15 grape tomatoes, sliced

1. Slice jalapeño peppers lengthwise, remove the seeds, and chop coarsely. Rub garlic around the inside of a medium saucepan. Discard garlic.

2. Add wine to the saucepan and cook over low heat. Don't allow wine to boil. When wine is warm, stir in lemon juice. Add cheeses, a handful at a time. Stir cheese continually in a sideways figure-eight pattern. Wait until cheese is completely melted before adding more. Don't allow cheese to boil.

3. In a small bowl, dissolve cornstarch in kirsch and then add to cheese, stirring. Turn up the heat to medium until mixture is just bubbling and starting to thicken. Add jalapeño peppers. Stir in curry powder.

4. Transfer to a fondue pot and set over the heat source set to low. Serve with bruschetta cubes and grape tomatoes for dipping.

Havarti with Stilton Swirl Fondue

Serves 6

A feast for the taste buds and the eyes! When the crumbled blue-veined Stilton is stirred into this creamy Havarti fondue just before serving, it gives the fondue an interesting color and texture. Serve this fondue with fruit, shortbread, nuts, and ladyfingers.

Ingredients

1½ cups white dessert wine

Juice of 1 medium lemon

1 pound Havarti cheese, rind removed

1½ tablespoons cornstarch

3 tablespoons apple brandy

½ pound Stilton cheese, crumbled

1. In a medium heavy saucepan over medium heat, pour in wine. Add lemon juice. Bring mixture to a simmer.

2. In a food processor, grate Havarti. Add ¼ grated cheese to the simmering liquid and stir in a figure-eight pattern. Once that cheese has melted, add another ¼ to the saucepan. Keep stirring. Repeat until all Havarti is melted and mixture is hot but not boiling.

3. In a small bowl, dissolve cornstarch in apple brandy. Stir into Havarti mixture. Cook until just bubbly, and then reduce heat and simmer 1 additional minute.

4. Pour liquid into one or more fondue pots. Swirl crumbled Stilton into the fondue and keep warm over a heat source set to low. Serve.

Mixed Sausages with Red Pearl Onions in Beer Fondue

Serves 8

This dish is like Oktoberfest in a meal! The classic fall flavors of onions, sausages, and beer will delight your senses and your belly. Serve this dish with rolls, some dark bread, crisp sauerkraut, and your favorite mustards.

Ingredients

1 pound knackwurst

1 pound bratwurst

1 pound smoked duck sausage

2 cups peeled red pearl onions

4 cups pilsner-type beer

Juice of 1 medium lemon

¼ teaspoon Tabasco sauce

1. Cut sausages into 1" slices and place together on a serving platter or board. Mix onions with sausages on platter.

2. In a medium saucepan over medium-high heat, bring beer, lemon juice, and Tabasco to a boil. Pour hot beer into fondue pots, no more than half full. Set fondue pots over heat source set at low heat.

3. Encourage guests to use dipping forks to spear sausages with an onion and plunge into hot beer until sausage is hot and onion has begun to soften.

One Potato, Two Potato...

If you want, boiled potatoes would be an excellent addition to this fondue. Boiled potatoes have a wonderfully earthy, primal flavor that complements the richness of the sausages and the tartness of sauerkraut and mustards you serve this with.

Breakfast Fondue

Serves 6

This mixture of cheese and eggs is perfect for any time of the day. For extra flavor, garnish with grated Cheddar cheese and chopped bacon. Serve this with bread cubes or try pieces of ham, sausages, baby potatoes, or cooked radishes.

Ingredients

1 clove garlic, peeled and cut in half

1½ cups dry white wine

1 tablespoon lemon juice

¾ pound Gruyère cheese, finely diced

¾ pound Emmentaler cheese, finely diced

2 tablespoons Worcestershire sauce

⅛ teaspoon salt

⅛ teaspoon black pepper

2 medium green onions, minced

12 large eggs

1 teaspoon cornstarch

2 teaspoons water

1 medium loaf bread, toasted and cut into squares

1. Rub garlic around the inside of a medium saucepan. Discard garlic. Add wine to the pan and warm over medium-low heat. Don't allow wine to boil.

2. When wine is warm, stir in lemon juice. Add cheeses, a handful at a time. Stir cheese continually in a sideways figure-eight pattern. Wait until cheese is completely melted before adding more. Don't allow the fondue mixture to boil.

3. When cheese is melted, turn up the heat until it is just bubbling and starting to thicken. Stir in Worcestershire sauce, salt and pepper, and green onion.

4. Whisk in eggs and scramble.

5. In a small bowl, dissolve cornstarch in water and add to the mixture to thicken.

6. Transfer mixture to a fondue pot and set over the heat source on low heat. Serve with the toasted bread for dipping.

Champagne Fondue

Serves 4

Next time you want to break out the bubbly, try using it in fondue! This is a perfect recipe for celebrating special occasions such as New Year's Eve, Valentine's Day, or Tuesday! Serve any leftover Brie on crackers with the remainder of the champagne.

Ingredients

1 clove garlic, smashed, peeled, and cut in half

1 cup plus 2 tablespoons dry champagne, divided

2 teaspoons lemon juice

1 pound Brie, cut into cubes

2 teaspoons cornstarch

⅛ teaspoon ground nutmeg

1 medium baguette, cut into cubes

1. Rub garlic around the inside of a medium saucepan. Discard garlic. Add 1 cup champagne to the saucepan and warm over medium-low heat. Don't allow it to boil.

2. When champagne is warm, stir in lemon juice. Add cheese, a few cubes at a time. Stir cheese continually in a sideways figure-eight pattern. Wait until cheese is completely melted before adding more. Don't allow the fondue mixture to boil.

3. In a small bowl, dissolve cornstarch in remaining 2 tablespoons champagne. When cheese is melted, add dissolved cornstarch. Turn up the heat until it is just bubbling and starting to thicken. Stir in nutmeg.

4. Transfer to a fondue pot and set over the heat source set to low. Serve with baguette cubes for dipping.

Champagne and Chocolate—a Big No-No

As romantic as it sounds, a bottle of fine champagne isn't the best way to finish off a romantic dessert fondue served over an open flame. Unfortunately, the acidity level in champagne clashes with sweet chocolate. If you do choose to pair champagne with chocolate, stick to the sweeter varieties such as demi-sec.

Raspberry Swirl Fondue

Serves 4

Sweet and savory, this bright and cheery dish is the best of both worlds. The juicy texture and delicate flavor of raspberries nicely complement sweet and creamy Havarti cheese. Serve this with the suggested baguette cubes or you can also try breadsticks or colorful fruits like grapes, apples, or raspberries.

Ingredients

1½ cups fresh raspberries

4 teaspoons lime juice

4 teaspoons sugar

¾ cup dry white wine, divided

2 teaspoons lemon juice

1 pound Havarti cheese, diced

4 teaspoons cornstarch

5 teaspoons water

1 medium baguette, cut into cubes

1. In a blender or food processor, process raspberries, lime juice, and sugar until smooth.

2. In a medium saucepan over medium-low heat, warm ½ cup wine. Don't allow wine to boil. Keep remaining ¼ cup wine warming in a separate small saucepan.

3. When wine is warm, stir in lemon juice. Add cheese, a handful at a time. Stir cheese continually in a sideways figure-eight pattern. Wait until cheese is completely melted before adding more. Don't allow the fondue mixture to boil.

4. When cheese is melted, stir in raspberry purée and heat through.

5. In a small bowl, dissolve cornstarch in water and then add to cheese, stirring. Turn up the heat until it is just bubbling and starting to thicken.

6. Add remaining ¼ cup wine if necessary. Transfer to a fondue pot and set over the heat source on low heat. Serve with baguette cubes for dipping.

Lump Crab and Cream Cheese Fondue

Serves 12

Here's a fondue variation of a favorite hot dip that will wow at any party. For an added twist, just add 1 (9-ounce) pack of frozen artichoke hearts, thawed and finely chopped, to the mix. Serve this fondue with pieces of brioche, croissants, and raw vegetables.

Ingredients

12 ounces cream cheese

1¼ cups heavy cream

½ cup mayonnaise

1 pound lump crabmeat

¼ cup grated Parmesan cheese

¼ cup finely chopped green onion

¼ cup finely chopped parsley

⅛ teaspoon black pepper

2 tablespoons sherry

1. In a medium saucepan over low heat, warm cream cheese and cream until cream cheese is melted and mixture is smooth. Increase heat to medium. When mixture is bubbly, quickly whisk in mayonnaise. Reduce heat.

2. Stir in crabmeat, Parmesan, green onion, parsley, and pepper. Stir in sherry.

3. Pour mixture into a fondue pot and place over heat source on low heat. Serve.

An Extravagant Gesture

The fastest way to make guests feel indulged and coddled is by show-casing luxury ingredients (lump crabmeat, lobster, filet mignon) on your table. Prepare them simply and wait for the compliments.

Fried Fish Fondue

Serves 8

In this recipe you create breaded fish pieces that you and your guests can fry in the fondue pots and enjoy right away. The combination of coatings—cornmeal, flour, and panko bread crumbs—gives this fish a flavorful, crunchy coating that can't be achieved with flour or cornmeal alone.

Ingredients

2 cups all-purpose flour, divided

1 tablespoon salt

1 teaspoon cayenne pepper

1 teaspoon black pepper

½ teaspoon garlic powder

3 pounds catfish or grouper fillets, cut into 1" cubes

2 medium eggs

3 tablespoons half and half

½ cup cornmeal

1 cup corn flour

1 cup panko bread crumbs

5 cups peanut oil

1. In a medium bowl, combine 1 cup flour with salt, cayenne pepper, black pepper, and garlic powder. Stir with a whisk. Toss fish cubes in seasoned flour and lightly coat.

2. In a large bowl, whisk together eggs and half and half. In a deep baking dish, mix together cornmeal, corn flour, bread crumbs, and remaining cup flour.

3. Dip fish cubes in egg mixture, then coat with crumb mixture and place in a shallow casserole or serving platter. Cover and refrigerate until ready to use.

4. Fill one or two fondue pots with oil no more than ⅓ full. Heat to 350°F. Guests should skewer fish with fondue forks, then place in oil until brown and crispy, about 3–4 minutes.

Bacon-Wrapped Shrimp

Serves 6

The dill adds a bit of brightness to the salty flavor of the bacon, making this a simple but delightful dish. Serve this as an appetizer at your next cocktail party.

Ingredients

18 large raw tiger shrimp,
   peeled and deveined, tails on

6 slices bacon

1/3 cup fresh baby dill, divided

4 cups canola oil, or as needed

1/4 cup lemon juice

1/4 cup sugar

1. Rinse shrimp in cold water, drain thoroughly, and pat dry.

2. Remove any excess fat off bacon and cut each piece into thirds. Take about 1/4 teaspoon baby dill and place on shrimp. Wrap a piece of bacon around shrimp two to three times. Continue with remainder of shrimp. Place on a serving platter on the table.

3. Add oil to the fondue pot, making sure it is not more than half full. Heat the pot on the stove over medium-high heat. When oil is hot, move the fondue pot to the table and place over heat source at low heat.

4. Use dipping forks to spear shrimp. Cook in hot oil about 30 seconds. Serve with remaining dill, lemon juice, and sugar for dipping.

How to Devein Shrimp

The purpose of deveining a shrimp is to remove the gray intestinal tract running down its back. The tract is frequently filled with dirt or sand, which can add an unpleasant gritty taste. To devein, peel the shrimp and cut a slit down the center of its back. Pull out the vein. Use the same procedure to devein prawns.

Caribbean Butterflied Shrimp

Serves 2

With banana, rum, lime, and coconut flavors, this dish will make you feel like you're in the Caribbean! Use mild or strong curry powder, depending on your preference for heat.

Ingredients

12 large raw shrimp, peeled and deveined, tails on

1 tablespoon butter

2 cloves garlic, smashed and peeled

½ cup light cream

4 teaspoons lime juice

½ cup rum

¼ teaspoon curry powder

1 cup sweetened coconut flakes

1 firm medium banana, peeled and cut into ½" slices

1. Rinse shrimp in cold water and pat dry with paper towels. To butterfly shrimp, make an incision lengthwise down the back. Cut down as deeply as possible without cutting through. Halfway down the back, make two parallel cuts on the left and right of the incision. Flatten down the four quarters, and place on a large serving platter.

2. In a medium saucepan, melt butter over low heat. Add garlic and cook in melting butter 2–3 minutes. Add cream and lime juice. Carefully add rum. Stir in curry powder.

3. Transfer the mixture to a fondue pot and set over the heat source at low heat at the table. Use dipping forks to spear shrimp and cook in the fondue until they change color. Dip into coconut flakes.

4. When shrimp are gone, dip banana in the fondue and then dip it into coconut flakes.

> **Use Real Cream!**
>
> *Half and half is made by combining cream with milk, and it can curdle at high temperatures. While it's safe to use in chocolate dessert fondues, which never reach the boiling point, use real cream for recipes like this one.*

Halibut and Lobster Tail Wine Fondue

Serves 8

This dish feels and tastes luxurious, but it doesn't have to break the bank. Rather than traditional (and sometimes expensive) Maine lobster tails, try using less expensive spiny or rock lobster tails in this dish.

Ingredients

3 pounds halibut fillets, cut into 1" cubes

8 small lobster tails, shelled, cut into 1" slices

4 cups Chablis

1 bouquet garni (see sidebar)

½ cup butter, melted

2 cloves garlic, peeled and pressed

2 tablespoons lemon juice

½ teaspoon chopped fresh tarragon

⅛ teaspoon salt

⅛ teaspoon black pepper

1. Place halibut and lobster on a serving plate with skewers. Encourage guests to thread one piece of each on skewers.

2. In a medium saucepan over medium heat, heat Chablis with bouquet garni until just starting to bubble. Discard herbs. Pour hot wine into fondue pots. Guests can dip fish and lobster skewers in pot until seafood is just opaque.

3. In a medium bowl, combine melted butter, garlic, lemon juice, tarragon, salt, and pepper. Pour into small dishes for dipping sauce.

> ### What Is Bouquet Garni?
> *Bouquet garni is a small cache of aromatic herbs either tied together with string or placed in a cheesecloth pouch. Usual ingredients include bay leaves, thyme sprigs, and parsley sprigs. Some cooks add celery and green onion to the mix. Make your own or buy it already packaged.*

Queso Chili con Carne

Serves 12

Skip the trip to your favorite Mexican food restaurant and get your queso fix at home in your fondue pot! Seasoned with cayenne pepper, this cheesy favorite is perfect for when you are looking for a little bit of spice in your night. Serve with tortilla chips for delicious homemade nachos or try cauliflower, celery, or colorful bell pepper slices to get in some added vegetables!

Ingredients

1 cup half and half

12 ounces Monterey jack cheese, shredded

12 ounces Manchego cheese, shredded

4 ounces sharp Cheddar cheese, shredded

1 (15-ounce) can chili-seasoned tomato sauce

1 pound ground beef, cooked and drained

2 medium green onions, chopped

⅛ teaspoon cayenne pepper

1. In a large saucepan over medium heat, heat half and half. Add cheeses in four batches, stirring each batch in a figure-eight motion until melted.

2. Stir in tomato sauce and ground beef.

3. Add green onions and cayenne. Cook over medium heat until thick and bubbly.

4. Spoon into fondue pot and place over heat source on low heat. Serve.

Savory Scallop and Sake Fondue

Serves 3

Scallops cooked in sake is a delicious treat you don't want to miss out on. For this dish you'll want to go with sea scallops, not bay scallops. Sea scallops are the large white scallops, while bay scallops are much smaller and have a creamy color.

Ingredients

⅓ cup vegetable oil

1 tablespoon sesame oil

¼ cup soy sauce

2 tablespoons lime juice

1 tablespoon maple syrup

2 medium green onions, chopped

1 pound sea scallops

2 cups sake

1. In a medium bowl, combine vegetable oil, sesame oil, soy sauce, lime juice, maple syrup, and green onion. Pour into a resealable plastic bag. Place scallops in bag and refrigerate 6 hours or overnight.

2. Remove scallops from marinade and place on a platter with fondue forks or skewers.

3. Heat sake to simmering in a small saucepan and then pour into a fondue pot over heat source at low heat, allowing pot to be halfway full.

4. Skewer scallops and cook in sake until opaque.

Make Your Own Marinade

It's easy to create your own marinade recipe. The one essential ingredient in a marinade is an acid. Acids such as wine, lemon juice, and vinegar act to tenderize the meat. Vegetable oil is frequently added to spread the flavor more quickly, but it isn't essential. The remaining ingredients are up to you! Feel free to experiment by adding your favorite herbs, spices, or even peanut butter.

Thai Seafood Hot Pot Broth

Serves 8

This fragrant broth resembles a thin Thai curry, with lemongrass and lime simmering in rich coconut milk. Round out this dish by serving it with a side of jasmine rice.

Ingredients

2 tablespoons vegetable oil

1 tablespoon green Thai curry paste

6 cups fish stock

2 cups coconut milk

1 medium onion, peeled and sliced

4 cloves garlic, peeled and minced

1 stalk lemongrass, cut in 1" pieces

Juice of 2 medium limes

1 teaspoon lime zest

⅓ cup fresh basil ribbons

3 pounds large shrimp, peeled

1 pound scallops

1 pound sea bass fillets, cut in 1" cubes

2 pounds cleaned baby mussels

2 cups diced eggplant

2 cups diced zucchini

2 cups sliced red bell pepper

½ cup chopped cilantro

1. In a large saucepan, heat vegetable oil over medium-high heat. Add curry paste and cook, stirring constantly for 1 minute. Add stock, coconut milk, onion, garlic, lemongrass, lime juice, lime zest, and basil. Stir well to dissolve curry paste.

2. Bring to a boil, and then quickly reduce heat to medium-low. Simmer 10–15 minutes.

3. Arrange shrimp, scallops, and sea bass on a platter. Place mussels in the shells in a bowl. Arrange eggplant, zucchini, and bell pepper on another platter. Sprinkle chopped cilantro over the seafood and veggie platters.

4. Ladle hot coconut milk broth into one or more fondue pots and set over heat source at low heat. Provide guests with wire strainers for dipping seafood and veggies in the broth. Fish and shellfish should be cooked briefly, just until the outside becomes opaque.

Mongolian Hot Pot Broth

Serves 8

If you prefer, chicken or venison can be substituted for the lamb, and if you don't have sake you can use white wine.

Ingredients

½ cup plus 2 tablespoons soy sauce, divided

⅓ cup dark sesame oil

1 tablespoon lemon juice

1 teaspoon grated ginger

1 teaspoon sesame seeds

2 pounds beef flank steak, thinly sliced

2 pounds boneless lamb loin, thinly sliced

2 cups trimmed snow peas

16 medium green onions

1 large head Chinese cabbage, coarsely shredded

8 cups beef broth

3 cloves garlic, peeled and pressed

¼ cup sake

1 teaspoon rice vinegar

1 pound bean thread noodles

1. In a large bowl, whisk together ½ cup soy sauce, sesame oil, lemon juice, ginger, and sesame seeds. Separately, toss beef and lamb in the marinade and arrange meats on a serving platter. Cover and refrigerate until ready to serve.

2. Arrange snow peas, green onions, and cabbage on a separate platter. Cover until ready to serve.

3. In a medium saucepan over medium-high heat, combine broth, garlic, sake, remaining soy sauce, and vinegar. Bring to a boil. Reduce heat and simmer 10 minutes.

4. Pour broth into one or more fondue pots and place over heat sources at low heat. Keep leftover broth warm on the stove. Have guests use chopsticks or hot pot strainers to cook meats and vegetables in fondue, about 1–2 minutes.

5. In a medium bowl, soak noodles in hot water for 10 minutes. When guests have cooked meats and veggies, add softened noodles to hot broth. Serve broth and noodles to guests in soup bowls.

Shabu-Shabu

Serves 6

Never heard of kombu? It's an edible kelp that is high in nutrients and is thought to help with a variety of things like digestion, thyroid problems, and even fighting cancer. This fondue uses the power of kombu in its broth and combines it with nutritious vegetables and sirloin steak. Serve this fondue with dipping sauces of your choice and rice.

Ingredients

8 cups water

2 (6") pieces kombu

2½ pounds sirloin steak

6 medium leeks

6 medium carrots, cut into chunks

3 cups button mushrooms

1 medium head Chinese cabbage, chopped

1 pound tofu, rinsed and diced

1. In a medium saucepan over medium-high heat, combine water and cleaned kombu. Bring liquid to a boil. Reduce heat and remove kombu. Maintain liquid at a simmer.

2. Slice sirloin across the grain in paper-thin slices. (Partial freezing can make slicing easier.) Arrange slices on serving platters.

3. Place vegetables on serving platters. Place tofu on serving platters.

4. Pour hot broth into one or more fondue pots and set pots over heat sources at low heat. Have guests use chopsticks to swish beef in broth to cook. Chopsticks or mesh strainers can be used for vegetables.

Chicken and Vegetables Bathed in Broth

Serves 4

This adaptation of a traditional Asian hot pot features a broth of chicken and ginger that adds a subtle warming flavor to your meat and veggies. After cooking them in the broth, you dip them in the Sour Cream and Mustard Dip (see sidebar) and chili sauce to add some heat and spice to each bite.

Ingredients

6 cups chicken broth

2 slices fresh ginger

2 (10-ounce) boneless, skinless chicken breasts, cut into thin strips

1 medium green bell pepper, seeded and cut into bite-sized pieces

1 medium red bell pepper, seeded and cut into bite-sized pieces

2 medium zucchini, cut into 1" pieces

2 medium stalks celery, cut into 1" pieces

1 medium tomato, cut into 6 wedges

2 portobello mushrooms, thinly sliced

Sour Cream and Mustard Dip (see sidebar)

½ cup hot chili sauce

1. In a medium saucepan over medium-high heat, heat broth with ginger slices and bring to a boil. Transfer enough broth to fill the fondue pot about ⅔ full. Set the fondue pot over the heat source on high heat, with enough heat to keep the broth simmering throughout the meal. (Keep the remaining broth warm on the stove to use as needed.)

2. Use dipping forks to spear chicken and vegetables and cook in the hot broth. Serve with Sour Cream and Mustard Dip and hot chili sauce for dipping.

> **Sour Cream and Mustard Dip**
>
> *This recipe yields 1¼ cups and can be used as a dip with seafood fondues, ham, raw vegetables, or crackers and breadsticks. In a small bowl, combine ½ medium green onion, minced, 1 cup sour cream, 2½ tablespoons Dijon mustard, 1 teaspoon lemon juice, and 1 teaspoon chopped parsley. Refrigerate, covered, until ready to serve.*

Pizza Fondue

Serves 6

All the Italian flavors of pizza—basil, oregano, tomatoes, and cheese—come together in this Pizza Fondue. For an added touch, sprinkle this fondue with shredded mozzarella cheese or finely sliced ham and mushrooms. Serve this fondue with soft breadsticks and hunks of pepperoni or salami, olives, and small whole pickles.

Ingredients

⅓ pound ground beef

2 tablespoons olive oil

1 medium yellow onion, peeled and chopped

¾ cup whole milk

1½ pounds Monterey jack cheese, shredded

1 cup tomato sauce

¼ teaspoon dried basil

¼ teaspoon dried oregano

½ pound Italian salami, sliced

20 black olives

Pickles

Soft Italian breadsticks

1. In a medium skillet over medium heat, brown the ground beef. Drain and set aside.

2. In a medium saucepan, heat oil over medium-low heat. Add onion and sauté until it is tender, about 5 minutes. Add milk and warm.

3. Add cheese a handful at a time. Stir cheese continually in a sideways figure-eight pattern. Wait until cheese is completely melted before adding more. Don't allow the fondue mixture to boil.

4. When cheese is nearly melted, add tomato sauce and ground beef and heat through. Turn up the heat until the fondue is just bubbling and starting to thicken. Add basil and oregano. Transfer to a fondue pot and set over the heat source on low heat.

5. Serve with salami, olives, pickles, and breadsticks for dipping.

Classic Beef Bourguignonne

Serves 6

This dish requires you to make two famous French sauces for dipping, béarnaise sauce and hollandaise sauce. But before you turn the page in fright thinking that you'll be in the kitchen for hours making complicated French recipes, relax. This recipe gives you quick and easy options for creating the sauces that will elevate your bourguignonne to fondue heaven.

Béarnaise Sauce Ingredients

⅓ cup white wine vinegar

5 tablespoons white wine

1 tablespoon chopped shallot

2½ tablespoons chopped fresh tarragon

⅔ cup butter

4 large egg yolks

1¼ tablespoons chopped parsley

¼ teaspoon cayenne pepper

⅛ teaspoon salt

½ teaspoon sugar

Hollandaise Sauce Ingredients

2 tablespoons white wine vinegar

2 tablespoons lemon juice

2 tablespoons chopped fresh dill

½ cup butter

3 large egg yolks

⅛ teaspoon cayenne pepper

Fondue Ingredients

5 cups vegetable oil, or as needed

¼ cup hot chili powder

1¾ pounds beef sirloin, cut into ¾" cubes

1. **For béarnaise sauce:** Combine vinegar, wine, shallot, and tarragon in a small saucepan over medium heat. Heat until the sauce is reduced to ⅓ cup. Cool and strain by lining a funnel with cheesecloth and then straining the sauce through the funnel.

2. While white wine vinegar mixture is heating, melt butter in a small saucepan. Keep butter warm over low heat.

3. Place white wine vinegar mixture in the top of a double boiler, over water that is hot but not boiling. (If you don't have a double boiler, use a metal bowl placed over a saucepan half filled with simmering water.) Make sure the bottom of the top boiler does not touch the heated water. Slowly add egg yolks and warm butter, whisking constantly. When the mixture has thickened, whisk in parsley, cayenne, salt, and sugar. Whisk until the sauce has thickened.

4. Serve the sauce immediately or cover and refrigerate until ready to serve. If preparing ahead of time, the refrigerated sauce can be served warm or cold. If serving warm, reheat by placing the bowl containing the sauce inside another bowl filled with hot water. Stir briefly. This prevents the sauce from curdling.

5. **For hollandaise sauce:** In a small saucepan over low heat, warm vinegar, lemon juice, and chopped dill. In a separate small saucepan, melt butter and keep it hot without burning.

6. Place white wine vinegar mixture in a blender and process for about 10 seconds. Add egg yolks and cayenne pepper.

7. Pour butter into the blender and process on high speed for at least 40 seconds or until the sauce has thickened. (Note: If the sauce is not thick enough, place it in the top of a double boiler over hot, but not boiling, water, and whisk until thickened. Remove from the heat as soon as it's thickened.) Refrigerate until ready to serve.

8. **For fondue:** Add oil to the fondue pot, making sure it is not more than half full. Heat the pot on the stove over medium-high heat.

9. When oil is hot, move the fondue pot to the table and set over the heat source at low heat. Set out the béarnaise sauce, hollandaise sauce, and ground hot chili powder in small bowls. Use dipping forks to spear beef cubes. Cook briefly in the hot oil and then dip into the sauces or seasoning.

Chicken Egg Rolls

Yields 10 egg rolls

Why wait for Chinese food takeout when you can make your own healthier version at home? You can use either white or dark chicken meat in these egg rolls. Use whichever you like best or even a combination of the two would work.

Ingredients

4 ounces chicken meat, chopped

1 teaspoon Chinese cooking wine

¼ teaspoon sesame oil, divided

2 teaspoons water

1 tablespoon plus 1 teaspoon oyster sauce

1 teaspoon soy sauce

½ teaspoon sugar

4 dried Chinese mushrooms

2 tablespoons plus 1 teaspoon grated carrot

1 tablespoon bamboo shoots, shredded

2 tablespoons plus 1 teaspoon finely diced red bell pepper

4 cups vegetable oil, or as needed

10 egg roll wrappers

4 tablespoons cornstarch mixed with 2 tablespoons water

1. In a medium bowl, combine chicken, wine, and a few drops sesame oil. Let this marinate 30 minutes in the refrigerator.

2. In a small bowl, mix together water, oyster sauce, soy sauce, and sugar. Set aside.

3. Soak mushrooms in warm water at least 20 minutes to soften. Squeeze out the excess water, remove the stems, and thinly slice. Add mushroom slices to a medium bowl and add grated carrot, bamboo shoots, and bell pepper. Mix together to combine.

4. Add 2 tablespoons vegetable oil to a medium frying pan over medium heat. When oil is hot, add chicken. Fry 8–10 minutes or until it changes color, and then add vegetables. Mix in the prepared sauce and bring to a boil. Drizzle with remaining sesame oil. Remove from heat and cool.

Recipe continued on next page

5. To prepare egg rolls, lay a wrapper in front of you so that it forms a square. Use your fingers to brush all the edges of wrapper with cornstarch mixture. Place a heaping tablespoon of filling in the middle. Fold the top of wrapper over the filling, fold the bottom half over the top, and seal the edges with more cornstarch and water. Seal the side edges, fold over, and seal again. Continue preparing the remainder of egg rolls.

6. Add remainder of vegetable oil to the fondue pot, making sure it is not more than half full. Heat the pot on the stove over medium-high heat. When oil is hot, move the fondue pot to the table and set over the heat source at low heat. Deep-fry egg rolls, two at a time, 5–7 minutes or until they turn golden. Drain and serve.

Vegetable Spring Rolls

Serves 6

Spring roll wrappers can be found in most supermarkets and are easy to work with.

Ingredients

4 dried Chinese mushrooms

1 cup fresh mung bean sprouts

2 tablespoons plus 1 teaspoon grated carrot

1 tablespoon shredded bamboo shoots

2 tablespoons plus 1 teaspoon finely diced red bell pepper

1 tablespoon plus 1 teaspoon oyster sauce

2 teaspoons water

½ teaspoon sugar

1 teaspoon soy sauce

5 cups vegetable oil, or as needed

8–10 spring roll wrappers

4 tablespoons cornstarch mixed with 2 tablespoons water

1. In a small bowl, soak mushrooms in warm water at least 20 minutes to soften. Squeeze out the excess water, remove the stems, and thinly slice.

2. In a medium bowl, mix mushrooms, mung bean sprouts, carrot, bamboo shoots, and pepper.

3. In a small bowl, mix together oyster sauce, water, sugar, and soy sauce. Set aside.

4. Heat 1½ tablespoons oil in a medium frying pan over medium-high heat. When oil is hot, add vegetables. Mix in the sauce and bring to a boil.

5. To prepare the spring rolls, lay a wrapper in front of you. Brush the edges of wrapper with cornstarch mixture. Place a tablespoon of filling in the middle. Roll up wrapper, tucking in the edges, and seal with more cornstarch and water. Prepare remaining spring rolls in the same way.

6. Add remaining oil to the fondue pot, filling it halfway. Heat the pot on the stove over medium-high heat. When oil is hot, move pot to the table and set over low heat.

7. Deep-fry spring rolls, two at a time, until they turn golden (3–4 minutes). Drain on paper towels.

Chicken in Pineapple-Orange Curry Fondue

Serves 8

This fondue smells heavenly while cooking; plus, it isn't too spicy for those with milder, but discerning, palates. The citrus notes in this dish complement the heat of the curry paste and the saltiness of the soy.

Ingredients

2 cups chicken broth

2 cups orange juice

2 cups pineapple juice

1 tablespoon Thai massaman curry paste

1 teaspoon soy sauce

1 (10-ounce) can coconut milk

4 (7-ounce) boneless, skinless chicken breasts, cut into bite-sized pieces

3 medium green bell peppers, seeded and cut into bite-sized pieces

1 medium fresh pineapple, peeled and cut into bite-sized pieces

1 large onion, peeled and cut into bite-sized pieces

1. In a large saucepan over medium heat, bring chicken broth, orange juice, pineapple juice, curry paste, and soy sauce to a boil. Stir until paste is dissolved and let simmer 3 minutes. Reduce heat slightly and add coconut milk. Simmer 10 minutes.

2. Thread chicken, peppers, pineapple, and onion onto skewers, alternating chicken and pineapple with vegetables. Place skewers on a serving platter.

3. Pour hot curry mixture into one or more fondue pots and place pots over heat sources on low heat. Have guests hold skewers in the hot curry broth until chicken is opaque and cooked through.

Deep-Fried Wieners

Serves 6

Why wait for a carnival or state fair to come to your town when you can have your own Deep-Fried Wieners in your fondue pot at home? These little treats are like those delicious, greasy, salty corn dogs you get at midways. Serve these wieners with your favorite dipping sauces like sweet-and-sour sauce, honey mustard, or Worcestershire sauce.

Basic Batter Ingredients

1 teaspoon baking soda

1 cup all-purpose flour

2 tablespoons vegetable oil

⅛ teaspoon black pepper

½ teaspoon cayenne pepper

1 cup soda water

Wieners Ingredients

12 small wieners

¼ cup cornstarch

4 cups vegetable oil, or as needed

1. **For batter:** In a medium bowl, sift baking soda into flour. Stir in vegetable oil, black pepper, and cayenne pepper.

2. Slowly add soda water until batter is similar in texture to pancake batter. Feel free to adjust the amount of water or flour to obtain the right consistency. Allow the batter to rest in the refrigerator 30 minutes before using.

3. **For wieners:** Dust wieners lightly with cornstarch. Place a skewer or stick through each wiener and place on a serving tray at the table.

4. Add oil to the fondue pot, making sure it is not more than half full. Heat the pot on the stove over medium-high heat. When oil is hot, move the fondue pot to the table and set it over the heat source on high heat.

5. Invite guests to coat wieners in the batter and then cook in the hot oil until the batter turns golden brown. Drain on paper towels if desired.

Meatballs with Basil

Serves 4

Filling and satisfying, not to mention beautiful, these meatballs are a showstopper. The spicy yogurt adds a creamy, spicy hit that perfectly rounds out the meal.

Ingredients

8 ounces ground beef

4 fresh basil leaves, chopped

¼ teaspoon celery salt

1 tablespoon chopped yellow onion

2 tablespoons ground cardamom

2 teaspoons ground coriander

1 teaspoon ground cumin

2 teaspoons ground cinnamon

¼ cup plain low-fat yogurt

¼ cup sour cream

4½ cups canola oil, or as needed

1. In a large bowl, using your hands, mix together ground beef, basil leaves, celery salt, and onion. Shape ground beef mixture into nine meatballs the size of golf balls.

2. In a small bowl, blend together cardamom, coriander, cumin, and cinnamon.

3. In a separate small bowl, combine yogurt and sour cream. Add 2 teaspoons of the blended spices to yogurt mixture. Store remainder of spice mixture in a sealed container to use another time.

4. Add oil to the fondue pot, making sure it is not more than half full. Heat the pot on the stove over medium-high heat.

5. When oil is hot, move the fondue pot to the table and set over the heat source on high heat. Using metal skewers with wooden handles, skewer the meatballs so that the skewer comes out the other side of the meatball. Cook the meatball in hot oil 4–5 minutes, until the meat is cooked through.

6. Serve with spiced yogurt mixture for dipping.

Chicken with Coconut Rice

Serves 8

Coconut milk and peanut are classic Thai flavors that are effortlessly showcased in this restaurant-quality fondue. Chicken cubes are perfect for this recipe, but any veggie will also taste just as good. Try broccoli, carrots, or cauliflower for a vegetarian version.

Ingredients

4 (7-ounce) boneless, skinless chicken breasts

3¼ cups coconut milk, divided

2 teaspoons fish sauce

5 teaspoons lime juice, divided

4 teaspoons brown sugar, divided

2 cloves garlic, peeled and crushed

2 tablespoons olive oil

½ small onion, peeled and chopped

2 cups long-grain rice

5 cups vegetable oil, or as needed

½ cup black pepper

Thai Peanut Sauce (see sidebar)

1. Use a knife to make cuts in the surface of chicken. Place chicken in a shallow glass dish.

2. In a small bowl, combine ¼ cup coconut milk, fish sauce, 1 teaspoon lime juice, 2 teaspoons brown sugar, and crushed garlic. Pour the marinade over chicken. Refrigerate chicken and marinate overnight. When ready to prepare, remove any excess marinade and cut chicken into bite-sized cubes.

3. In a large saucepan over low heat, heat olive oil. Add onion and cook until soft. Add rice and sauté 5 minutes until it turns shiny and is heated through.

4. In a medium bowl, combine 3 cups coconut milk, 4 teaspoons lime juice, and 2 teaspoons brown sugar. Add to rice. Bring rice to a boil, uncovered, over medium heat. Cover, turn down the heat, and boil until cooked through, about 20 minutes, stirring occasionally. Keep rice warm over low heat.

5. Add oil to the fondue pot, making sure it is not more than half full. Heat the pot on the stove over medium-high heat.

6. When oil is hot, move the fondue pot to the table and set over the heat source at low heat. Skewer chicken cubes so that the skewer goes right through the meat. Cook chicken cubes in hot oil for 2–3 minutes until they are browned and cooked through. Serve with freshly ground black pepper and Thai Peanut Sauce for dipping. Eat with coconut rice.

Thai Peanut Sauce

This quick and easy peanut sauce can be whipped up in just a few minutes. Take ½ cup peanut butter, 4 tablespoons sugar, 4 teaspoons red curry paste, 3 tablespoons plus 1 teaspoon lime juice, ½ cup plus 2 tablespoons coconut milk, and 1 teaspoon nuoc mam fish sauce. In a blender or food processor, combine all ingredients except for fish sauce. Process until smooth. Remove and add to a small saucepan. Cook over low heat, stirring continuously, for at least 5 minutes. Stir in fish sauce. Serve warm or at room temperature.

Ham, Cheddar, and Walnut Fondue

Serves 4

This fondue takes on the classic combination of ham and cheese. The elements pair perfectly together, and the walnuts give it another level with their crunch. For a more romantic atmosphere, transfer the cooked mixture to a chocolate fondue pot and serve over an open flame. Try serving this with cubed baguette, fresh green beans, or zucchini chips.

Ingredients

1 pound Cheddar cheese, finely diced

1½ tablespoons cornstarch

1 clove garlic, smashed and peeled

2 tablespoons butter

2 tablespoons chopped yellow onion

½ cup sour cream

1 teaspoon lemon juice

1 cup chopped cooked ham

2 tablespoons chopped walnuts

1 medium baguette, cut into cubes

1. In a medium bowl, toss Cheddar with cornstarch and set aside.

2. Rub garlic around the inside of a medium saucepan. Discard garlic. In the saucepan, melt butter over medium heat and add onion. Cook 2–3 minutes, and then stir in sour cream.

3. Stir in lemon juice. Add cheese, a handful at a time. Stir cheese continually in a sideways figure-eight pattern. Wait until cheese is completely melted before adding more. Don't allow the fondue mixture to boil.

4. After half the cheese has melted, stir in ½ cup ham. When cheese is completely melted, stir in remainder of ham. Add walnuts.

5. Transfer to a fondue pot and set over the heat source set to low heat. Serve with baguette cubes for dipping.

Pork "Satay" Fondue

Serves 4

Peanut sauce is like liquid gold, and when combined with coconut pork and shrimp, it's a flavor explosion! For extra flavor, you can reserve the coconut marinade, boil for 5 minutes, and use as a dipping sauce with the shrimp.

Ingredients

2 teaspoons salt

12 large shrimp, peeled and deveined

2 cloves garlic, smashed, peeled, and minced

1 cup coconut milk

2 tablespoons plus 2 teaspoons lime juice

1 tablespoon plus 1 teaspoon red curry paste

3 teaspoons brown sugar

1½ pounds pork tenderloin, cut into 1"-thick cubes

5 cups vegetable oil, or as needed

Thai Peanut Sauce (see Chicken with Coconut Rice recipe in this part)

1. Dissolve salt in a medium bowl filled with 3 cups warm water. Soak shrimp in water 5 minutes. Drain.

2. In a medium bowl, combine garlic with coconut milk and lime juice. Stir in red curry paste and brown sugar.

3. Lay out pork cubes in a shallow glass dish. Pour just over half of coconut milk marinade over pork cubes. Refrigerate and marinate pork 1 hour.

4. Mix remaining marinade with shrimp and marinate 15 minutes. Remove any excess marinade from pork and shrimp.

5. Add oil to the fondue pot, making sure it is not more than half full. Heat the pot on the stove over medium-high heat. When oil is hot, move the fondue pot to the table and set it over the heat source. Keep the heat high.

6. Use dipping forks to spear pork and shrimp. Cook in hot oil—shrimp will cook more quickly than pork will. Serve with Thai Peanut Sauce for dipping.

Fried Potato Sticks

Serves 4

Potatoes were just made to be fried! This simple dish makes a filling snack or side dish. You can even serve these for breakfast!

Ingredients

4 large potatoes, peeled

5 cups vegetable oil, or as needed

¼ teaspoon black pepper

¼ teaspoon white pepper

1. Fill a medium stockpot with water and set over medium-low heat. Boil potatoes in it about 15 minutes until they can be pierced with a fork but are not too soft. Drain thoroughly, and cut lengthwise into pieces approximately ¾" thick.

2. Add oil to the fondue pot, making sure it is not more than half full. Heat the pot on the stove over medium-high heat. When oil is hot, move the fondue pot to the table and set over the heat source. Keep the heat on high.

3. Using a dipping fork, dip potato slices briefly into oil. Drain on paper towels or a tempura rack. Season with black or white pepper before eating.

Tempura Veggie Skewers with Ginger Soy Sauce

Serves 6

In this recipe you'll be making your own tempura vegetables—no need to order out! You'll make a simple batter that you and your guests can dip flavorful vegetables in and then fry to crispy perfection. You can buy ginger-flavored soy sauce to replace the fresh ginger in this recipe.

Ingredients

2 cups broccoli florets

2 cups cauliflower florets

2 cups small white mushrooms

2 cups sliced red bell pepper

3 large eggs

1 cup ice water

1 teaspoon salt

1 cup all-purpose flour

5 cups peanut oil

1 tablespoon sesame oil

1 cup soy sauce

2 tablespoons grated fresh ginger

1. Arrange vegetables on skewers, with two to three pieces on each, separated by bell pepper strips. Place skewers on a serving platter.

2. In a medium bowl, beat together eggs, water, salt, and flour. Cover and refrigerate until ready to use. Divide batter into two serving bowls for easy dipping.

3. Heat peanut oil in one or more fondue pots over medium-high heat. Pots should not be more than $\frac{1}{3}$ full.

4. In a small bowl, combine sesame oil, soy sauce, and ginger. Divide into six dipping bowls for guests.

5. Guests should dip veggie skewers in batter, then immediately dip into hot fondue pot. Fry in hot oil until batter is brown and crispy. Dip in ginger soy sauce and enjoy.

Fried Mushrooms

Serves 6

Because they become juicy and delicious when heated, cooked mushrooms don't require any extra seasoning. They are perfect all on their own! Serve these little bites as an appetizer or side dish to your favorite meals.

Ingredients

30 button mushrooms

4½ cups vegetable oil, or as needed

1. Cut mushrooms into slices approximately ½" thick.

2. Add oil to the fondue pot, making sure it is not more than half full. Heat the pot on the stove over medium-high heat.

3. When oil is hot, move the fondue pot to the table, set on the heat source, and maintain the heat at medium-high. Use a dipping fork to cook mushroom slices briefly in hot oil until golden. Drain on paper towels or a tempura rack.

Spinach and Artichoke Fondue

Serves 4

Spinach and artichokes—those key ingredients in so many delicious dips—are presented here in a cheesy, gooey, fantastic fondue. This fondue tastes great with French bread chunks and broccoli florets, but don't be afraid to try other options such as rye, pumpernickel, or tortilla chips.

Ingredients

½ cup shredded Gruyère cheese

¼ cup shredded Parmesan cheese

1 teaspoon all-purpose flour

⅓ cup white wine

1 tablespoon minced garlic

¾ cup chopped baby spinach

⅓ cup drained and chopped artichoke hearts

2 ounces cream cheese

1. In a medium bowl, combine Gruyère and Parmesan cheeses and sprinkle with flour. Toss to evenly coat and set aside.

2. In a medium saucepan over medium-high heat, add wine and garlic. Once it starts to boil, add spinach and artichokes; stir until spinach wilts.

3. Stir in shredded cheese mixture. Add cream cheese and keep stirring until cheeses are melted completely.

4. Transfer to a fondue pot and set over the heat source on low heat. Serve.

Indian Curried Lamb

Serves 4

Lamb and yogurt make a perfect combination. Here you'll cook lamb cubes to perfection in your fondue pot and serve with the special yogurt dip. For best results, make the spiced yogurt dip at least one day ahead of time to allow the flavors to blend.

Ingredients

2 tablespoons cardamom seeds, crushed

2 teaspoons ground coriander

4 teaspoons ground cumin, divided

2 teaspoons ground cinnamon

1¼ cups plain low-fat yogurt, divided

¼ cup sour cream

3 teaspoons curry powder

1 teaspoon black pepper

1 teaspoon turmeric

1½ pounds lean lamb

4 medium potatoes

1 tablespoon lemon juice

1 medium red bell pepper, seeded and cut into cubes

1 medium green bell pepper, seeded and cut into cubes

1 medium tomato, chopped

5 cups canola oil, or as needed

Recipe continued on next page

1. In a small bowl, blend together cardamom, coriander, 1 teaspoon cumin, and cinnamon.

2. In a separate small bowl, combine ¼ cup of yogurt with sour cream. Add 2 teaspoons of spice mixture to yogurt and sour cream. Store remainder of spice mixture in a sealed container to use another time. Refrigerate yogurt dressing until needed.

3. In a small bowl, blend together curry powder, remaining cumin, black pepper, and turmeric. Rub into lamb. Cut lamb into bite-sized cubes.

4. In a large stockpot over medium-low heat, boil potatoes about 15 minutes until they can be pierced with a fork but are not too soft.

5. In a medium bowl, stir lemon juice into remaining 1 cup yogurt. Add peppers and chopped tomato to yogurt and refrigerate until ready to serve.

6. Add oil to the fondue pot, making sure it is not more than half full. Heat the pot on the stove over medium-high heat. When oil is hot, move the fondue pot to the table and set over the heat source. Keep the heat high.

7. Use dipping forks to spear lamb cubes. Cook in hot oil until browned. Serve with the spiced yogurt mixture for dipping. Serve with boiled potatoes and pepper, tomato, and yogurt salad on the side.

Lamb Kebabs with Sun-Dried Tomato Bruschetta

Serves 4

Delicate olive oil enhances the Mediterranean flavors of tomatoes, mint, and garlic in this dish. Don't forget to make the Yogurt and Dill Dressing; it really adds to the meal.

Ingredients

1 medium baguette, cut into ½" slices

1 clove garlic, smashed, peeled, and cut in half

2 cups oil-packed sun-dried tomatoes, drained and chopped

4¼ cups olive oil, divided

1¾ pounds lean lamb, cut into bite-sized cubes

¼ cup fresh mint leaves

Yogurt and Dill Dressing (see sidebar)

1. Broil one side of baguette slices. Rub garlic over the toasted side. Spread tomatoes over the other side and drizzle with ¼ cup olive oil. Return to oven and broil the untoasted side. Set aside.

2. Place lamb on a serving platter surrounded by mint leaves.

3. Add about 4 cups oil to the fondue pot, making sure it is not more than half full. Heat the pot on the stove over medium-high heat. When oil is hot, move the fondue pot to the table and set over the heat source. Keep the heat high.

4. Use dipping forks to spear lamb cubes. Cook in hot oil until browned. Serve with Yogurt and Dill Dressing for dipping and the bruschetta on the side.

> **Yogurt and Dill Dressing**
>
> *To make, combine 1 cup low-fat yogurt, 1 tablespoon plus 1 teaspoon lemon juice, 1 tablespoon chopped fresh baby dill, 1 sprig fresh thyme leaves, stem removed, and 1½ teaspoons Dijon mustard in a small bowl. Refrigerate, covered, until ready to serve.*

Sweet Goat Cheese
with Roasted Red Peppers

Serves 6

Roasted red peppers and creamy goat cheese work so well together, and this dish takes advantage of that to create a fondue you won't want to share! Did you know the first mention of grated goat's cheese melted in wine can be traced back to Homer's Iliad? *So this dish is not only delicious but makes you more literary too!*

Ingredients

3 medium red bell peppers

2 medium yellow bell peppers

1 medium orange bell pepper

1 teaspoon balsamic vinegar

1 teaspoon olive oil

1 clove garlic, smashed, peeled, and cut in half

1½ cups dry white wine

1 tablespoon lemon juice

1½ pounds goat cheese, crumbled

1 tablespoon cornstarch

3 tablespoons kirsch

2 tablespoons chopped fresh tarragon

1 medium loaf stale bread

¼ cup olive oil

1. Preheat oven to 400°F.

2. Place peppers side down (not standing up) on a broiling pan. Brush top side of peppers with balsamic vinegar. Turn over and brush other side with olive oil. Broil peppers about 20 minutes, turning frequently, until the skins are blackened and charred.

3. Place peppers in a sealed plastic bag. Leave peppers in the bag at least 10 minutes. Remove from the bag and peel off the skins. Remove the stems and the seeds. Cut into cubes or lengthwise into strips. Set aside.

4. Rub garlic around the inside of a medium saucepan. Discard garlic. Add wine to the pan and warm over medium-low heat. Don't allow wine to boil.

5. When wine is warm, stir in lemon juice. Add cheese, a handful at a time, and stir continuously in a sideways figure-eight pattern. Wait until cheese is completely melted before adding more. Don't allow the fondue mixture to boil.

6. When cheese is melted, dissolve cornstarch in kirsch in a small bowl and then add to cheese, stirring. Turn the heat up until the fondue is just bubbling and starting to thicken. Stir in fresh tarragon leaves. Transfer to a fondue pot and set over the heat source at low heat.

7. Toast bread and drizzle a small amount of olive oil around the edges. Cut into cubes.

8. Serve the fondue with peppers as a side dish and bread for dipping.

Falafel Fondue

Serves 6

Crispy, warm falafels are perfect for a party appetizer, or make more and have them for dinner at home! Dried, soaked fava beans can be substituted for chickpeas in this popular Middle Eastern snack. If you don't like or can't use peanut oil, you can substitute a combination of vegetable and olive oil.

Ingredients

2 cups chickpeas, soaked overnight and drained

1 medium yellow onion, peeled and finely chopped

$\frac{1}{4}$ cup minced parsley

$\frac{1}{4}$ cup minced cilantro

2 cloves garlic, peeled and pressed

1 teaspoon baking powder

$\frac{1}{2}$ teaspoon cumin

$\frac{1}{4}$ teaspoon sesame oil

$\frac{1}{8}$ teaspoon salt

$\frac{1}{8}$ teaspoon black pepper

5 cups peanut oil

Quick Tahini Dip (see sidebar)

1. Place chickpeas in a food processor with onion, parsley, cilantro, and garlic. Pulse a few times.

2. Add baking powder, cumin, sesame oil, salt, and pepper. Pulse until mixture forms a smooth paste.

3. Roll paste into firm 1" balls.

4. Heat oil in one or more fondue pots over high heat, taking care not to fill pots more than $\frac{1}{3}$ full. Guests can use fondue forks to skewer firm falafel balls, or use wire strainers to dip falafel in hot oil.

5. Cook until balls are brown and crisp, about 3–5 minutes. Dip in Quick Tahini Dip before eating.

> ### Quick Tahini Dip
> *Sesame tahini is a peanut butter–like paste that adds flavor to many Middle Eastern dishes. To make tahini sauce, season tahini with a clove of pressed garlic, lemon juice, salt, and pepper to taste in a small bowl. Stir until smooth. For a thinner sauce, add more lemon juice or a little warm water.*

Beef and Peppers with Clarified Butter

Serves 4

The horseradish cream in this dish brings a surprising bite of heat that adds to the meal, so don't leave it out. Try serving this fondue with some rice to round out the meal. For more variety, try adding 1 pound large shrimp to the mix.

Horseradish Cream Ingredients

½ cup whipping cream

2 tablespoons prepared horseradish

½ teaspoon lemon juice

1 teaspoon Worcestershire sauce

Mint and Cilantro Chutney Ingredients

⅓ cup chopped cilantro leaves

½ cup chopped mint leaves

3 tablespoons plain low-fat yogurt

1½ teaspoons lemon juice

1 tablespoon chopped red onion

1 teaspoon sugar

1 tablespoon dark raisins

⅛ teaspoon cayenne pepper

Fondue Ingredients

2 tablespoons butter

1 medium red onion, peeled and chopped

10 ounces clarified butter

1 cup vegetable oil

1½ pounds beef tenderloin, cut into cubes

2 medium red bell peppers, seeded and cut into chunks

1 medium green bell pepper, seeded and cut into chunks

10 small fresh mushrooms, cut in half

1. **For horseradish cream:** In a medium metal bowl, beat whipping cream until it stiffens. Stir in horseradish, lemon juice, and Worcestershire sauce. Cover and refrigerate until ready to serve.

2. **For mint and cilantro chutney:** Combine all ingredients in a blender or food processor and process until smooth. Cover and refrigerate until ready to serve.

3. **For fondue:** In a small skillet over medium heat, heat 2 tablespoons butter. Add onion and sauté until it is soft and translucent. Set aside.

4. Add clarified butter and oil to the fondue pot. Heat the pot on a stove element over medium-high heat. When oil is hot, move the fondue pot to the table, set over the heat source, and maintain the heat.

5. Use dipping forks to spear beef and vegetables. Cook mushroom slices briefly in hot oil until golden, and beef until it is cooked through. Cook peppers very briefly. Drain on paper towels or a tempura rack if desired.

6. Serve with horseradish cream for dipping. Eat with sautéed onions and prepared chutney.

Part Two

SWEET FONDUES

Dark Chocolate Fondue

Serves 4

Serve this rich fondue with chunks of vanilla cake or fresh fruit like raspberries and strawberries. The orange liqueur is optional if you'd prefer the fondue without it.

Ingredients

8 ounces dark chocolate, roughly chopped

1 cup whipping cream

1 tablespoon orange liqueur

1. In a medium metal bowl, combine chocolate and cream and place on top of a saucepan half filled with simmering water. Melt mixture over low to medium-low heat, stirring frequently. Make sure that it doesn't boil.

2. When chocolate is melted, stir in liqueur. Transfer mixture into a fondue pot and set over the heat source. Keep warm on low heat. Serve.

Chocolate, Chocolate, Chocolate Fondue

Serves 8

Because the chips melt slower than the chocolate, they provide a nice texture to the fondue that makes it different from a standard chocolate fondue. The best way to serve this fondue is with gravy ladles and bowls.

Ingredients

1 pound milk chocolate

1 cup heavy cream

2 cups semisweet chocolate chips

1 cup white chocolate chips

Angel food cake, cut into cubes

Sugar cookies

1. In a large saucepan over low heat, combine milk chocolate and cream. Warm, stirring constantly, until chocolate is melted and mixture is smooth. Remove from heat and stir in semisweet and white chocolate chips.

2. At this point, mixture can be divided over one or more fondue pots and placed on heat-safe table pads. Allow guests to ladle a small amount of fondue, including chips, into individual serving bowls.

3. Pass a platter of angel food cake cubes and sugar cookies for dunking.

> ### In the Chips
> *Supermarket shelves boast peanut butter chips, butterscotch chips, mint chips, orange chips, and several shades of chocolate chips. Candy chips melt very slowly—they're designed to hold their shape— which makes them tricky for fondue. It's best to use them as flavor chips in a smooth fondue of melted chocolate.*

Basic Chocolate Fondue

Serves 4

What could be better than a pot of melted chocolate? Not a lot! Are you looking for a creative way to serve fresh fruit or cake? Try this delicious Basic Chocolate Fondue. The liqueur in this recipe is optional, so feel free to eliminate it if you desire. Serve this delicious chocolate creation with cubes of pound cake and bright, colorful fruits like strawberries, raspberries, cherries, nectarines, pineapple, or melons.

Ingredients

1 cup whipping cream

8 ounces semisweet chocolate, broken into pieces

1 tablespoon liqueur

1 pound fresh fruit of your choice

Pound cake, cut into cubes

1. In a medium metal bowl, combine whipping cream and chocolate and place bowl on top of a saucepan half filled with simmering water. Melt mixture over low to medium-low heat, stirring frequently. Make sure that it doesn't boil.

2. When chocolate is melted, stir in liqueur. Transfer chocolate mixture into the fondue pot and set over the heat source. Keep warm over low heat.

3. Use dipping forks to dip fruit and cake into the fondue.

Strawberry Shortcake Fondue

Serves 6

Instead of fondue forks, you may want to give guests long-handled ice tea spoons for this dish. The amaretto in this fondue gives a slight almond flavor that makes this not your ordinary strawberry shortcake.

Ingredients

6 cups sliced strawberries

1 cup superfine sugar

1 tablespoon amaretto

6 cups sweetened whipped cream

½ cup strawberry syrup or chocolate sauce

2 dozen ladyfingers

1. In a medium bowl, combine strawberries and sugar. Toss well. Pour into a glass baking dish or shallow serving bowl. Cover and refrigerate at least 1 hour. After 1 hour, remove from refrigerator, sprinkle amaretto over berries, and stir well.

2. Smooth top of berries, then pile on whipped cream, covering berries. Drizzle strawberry syrup or chocolate sauce over whipped cream.

3. Serve with spoons and ladyfingers for dipping.

> **Sugar Soak**
> *Sprinkling sugar over peeled fruit draws liquid from the fruit, which dissolves the sugar. The resulting sugar syrup softens and flavors the fruit.*

Cinnamon Fondue

Serves 6

Warm cinnamon adds a touch of spice to this chocolate fondue. Adding the cinnamon after the fondue has been removed from the heating agent will help keep the chocolate from seizing up.

Ingredients

8 ounces semisweet chocolate

4 ounces unsweetened chocolate

1 cup heavy cream

1 teaspoon ground cinnamon

1 pound fresh strawberries, hulled

1. Break semisweet and unsweetened chocolate into pieces.

2. In a medium metal bowl, combine cream and chocolate and place bowl over a saucepan half filled with barely simmering water. Melt chocolate over low to medium-low heat, stirring constantly. Do not let mixture overheat. Add more cream if necessary.

3. When chocolate has melted, transfer the fondue mixture to the fondue pot and set over the heat source. Keep the fondue warm over low heat. Stir in cinnamon.

4. Serve with strawberries for dipping.

Pumpkin Cheesecake Fondue

Serves 2

All the cheesecake flavoring with none of the cheesecake work! This Pumpkin Cheesecake Fondue is warm, spicy, and full of fall flavorings. Scooping it up with biscotti and shortbread cookies still gives you the "crust" feel of a cheesecake, but the star of this dessert is the pumpkin and cream cheese filling. Make a larger batch of this recipe for a delicious and unique Thanksgiving dessert.

Ingredients

⅓ cup canned pumpkin

3 ounces cream cheese

⅓ cup heavy cream

2 tablespoons sugar

1 teaspoon pumpkin pie spice

Shortbread cookies

Almond biscotti

1. In a medium saucepan, combine pumpkin, cream cheese, heavy cream, and sugar. Cook over medium heat, stirring constantly.

2. When cream cheese has melted, stir in pumpkin pie spice. Heat mixture until bubbly, and then pour into a fondue pot.

3. Place over heat source on lowest setting and enjoy with shortbread cookies and biscotti for dipping.

Pecan Caramels Chocolate Fondue

Serves 6

The nuts make a nice surprise in this melted mélange. The caramel takes longer to melt than the chocolate, so stir this fondue carefully.

Ingredients

1 pound box chocolate-covered pecan caramel clusters

1 cup heavy cream

Sugar cookies

Apple chunks

1. In a small saucepan over low heat, add chocolate candies and cream. Melt chocolate into cream. Stir constantly until mixture is combined and candies have all melted.

2. Pour chocolate mixture into a fondue pot and place over heat source on lowest setting. Serve with sugar cookies and apple chunks for dipping.

Chocolate Truffles Fondue

Serves 6

This recipe is as simple as getting your favorite type of truffle and turning it into a fondue with a few simple ingredients. Boxes of truffles come in dark, light, or mixed varieties. Pick your favorite and go with it.

Ingredients

1 pound box chocolate truffles

$\frac{2}{3}$ cup heavy cream

Pound cake fingers

Banana slices

1. In a small saucepan over low heat, combine truffles with cream. Melt truffles into cream. Stir constantly until mixture is smooth and thick.

2. Pour chocolate mixture into a fondue pot and place over heat source on lowest setting. Have guests dip pound cake fingers and banana slices into the fondue.

S'mores Fondue

Serves 3

Give us s'more of this fondue! The addition of evaporated milk turns this classic campfire favorite into a tasty fondue. This recipe yields just over 1 cup but can easily be doubled. In addition to the suggested marshmallows try dipping whole graham crackers in this delectable dip!

Ingredients

½ cup evaporated milk

30 miniature marshmallows

¾ cup semisweet
  chocolate chips

⅔ cup graham cracker crumbs

25 regular-sized marshmallows,
  or as needed

1. In a medium metal bowl, combine evaporated milk and miniature marshmallows and place bowl on top of a saucepan half filled with simmering water. Stir frequently over low heat, making sure mixture doesn't come to a boil.

2. When marshmallows are melted, add chocolate chips. Melt chocolate over low to medium-low heat, stirring frequently and continuing to make sure mixture doesn't boil.

3. When chocolate is melted, stir in graham cracker crumbs. Transfer the fondue mixture to the fondue pot and set over the heat source. Keep the fondue warm over low heat.

4. Serve with marshmallows for dipping.

> **S'more, Please!**
> *A favorite snack of the Girl Scouts since the 1920s, s'mores are made by combining chocolate with graham crackers and marshmallows. The name "s'mores" is reputed to be a shortening of the phrase "give me some more."*

Expressive Espresso Fondue

Serves 8

Not only does this fondue have a taste of espresso but the look too! The whipped cream in this dish starts out cold and whipped very stiff. As it melts, it resembles the froth atop a cup of espresso.

Ingredients

1½ pounds semisweet chocolate

½ cup heavy cream

1 cup brewed espresso

2 tablespoons Kahlúa

4 cups lightly sweetened whipped cream

Biscotti

1. In a medium saucepan over low heat, combine chocolate with heavy cream. Melt chocolate into cream. Stir constantly until mixture is smooth and thick.

2. Stir in espresso and Kahlúa. Stir until completely blended.

3. Pour chocolate mixture into one or more fondue pots and place over heat source on lowest setting. Ladle a little cold whipped cream over the fondue right before serving with biscotti for dipping.

> ### Coffee Options
> *In a pinch, espresso powder can be used in this dish in place of brewed espresso. Add 1–2 tablespoons of powder and a little more cream to the simmering chocolate. The end product will taste a little different but still very good.*

Mocha-Mocha Java Fondue

Serves 8

With two kinds of chocolate, Godiva liqueur, and mocha coffee, this recipe is made for the chocolate lover! It features the smooth taste of mocha java coffee, but feel free to try this recipe with your favorite coffee blend. Serve this fondue with a variety of biscotti dippers for a real coffeehouse treat!

Ingredients

1½ pounds semisweet chocolate

1 cup plus 2 tablespoons heavy cream, divided

1 cup brewed mocha java coffee

¼ cup Godiva liqueur

¼ pound white chocolate

Biscotti

1. In a medium saucepan over low heat, combine semisweet chocolate with 1 cup cream. Melt chocolate into cream, stirring constantly until mixture is smooth and thick. Stir in coffee and Godiva liqueur.

2. In a small saucepan over low heat, combine 2 tablespoons cream and white chocolate. Melt and stir until smooth.

3. Pour dark chocolate mixture into one or more fondue pots and place over heat source on lowest setting.

4. With a knife, carefully swirl white chocolate into mixture and serve with biscotti for dipping.

> ### A Vintage Cup o' Joe
> *Mocha java coffee pairs mocha beans from Yemen or Ethiopia with beans grown in Java. The popular blend, with its distinctive smooth-sweet flavor profile, is more than 250 years old. Mocha refers to the name of an ancient Yemeni port.*

White Chocolate Raspberry Fondue

Serves 6

You'll want to look for a quality chocolate brand when shopping for white chocolate because it will definitely affect the taste—don't cheap out on this one! White chocolate mixed with raspberries makes for a beautiful-looking (and beautiful-tasting) fondue, and with the dark chocolate pound cake dippers, this one will be a stunning addition to your party table.

Ingredients

½ cup sugar

½ cup water

2 cups fresh or
   frozen raspberries

1 pound white chocolate

⅔ cup heavy cream

¼ cup Chambord liqueur

Dark chocolate pound cake cubes

1. In a medium saucepan over medium heat, combine sugar and water. Cook, stirring constantly, until sugar is dissolved and mixture begins to boil. Remove from heat and cool slightly.

2. In a blender, combine sugar mixture with raspberries. Pulse to a purée.

3. In a medium saucepan over low heat, combine white chocolate and cream. Warm, stirring constantly, until chocolate is melted and mixture is smooth. Pour raspberry purée through a strainer into the white chocolate mixture. Add Chambord and stir well.

4. Warm until white chocolate mixture is hot. Pour into one or more fondue pots and place over heat source at low heat. Serve with chocolate pound cake cubes for dipping.

Cinnamon Cocoa Latte Fondue

Serves 8

This fondue will remind you of your favorite fall blends from the local coffee shop. Sweet, spicy, and chocolaty, with just a hint of bitter from the coffee, this fondue is a delicious treat no matter what time of year. Cinnamon syrup can be found in the coffee aisle of most supermarkets.

Ingredients

1½ pounds milk chocolate

1 cup heavy cream

½ cup cinnamon syrup

½ cup strong brewed coffee

Assorted biscotti

1. In a medium saucepan over low heat, combine chocolate with cream. Melt chocolate into cream. Stir constantly until mixture is smooth and thick.

2. Add syrup and coffee and stir until completely blended.

3. Pour chocolate mixture into one or more fondue pots and place over heat source on lowest setting. Serve with assorted biscotti for dipping.

Biscotti

Biscotti get their characteristic crunch from being baked twice. First, the dough is formed into a wide log and baked. Then the log is sliced and the slices are baked again. The resulting cookie is perfect for dunking in coffee or fondue and will stay fresh in a sealed container for weeks.

Creamy Caramel Fondue

Serves 6

In addition to the popcorn and marshmallow dippers, apple slices, pineapple slices, and crispy rice cereal treats all go particularly well with this recipe. This four-ingredient fondue could not be easier to make but tastes like you worked all day over a boiling pot with your candy thermometer!

Ingredients

2 cups sugar

1 cup evaporated milk

4 tablespoons corn syrup

4 tablespoons butter

6 cups any combination of marshmallows, sliced fruit, and/or popcorn

1. In a medium saucepan, combine sugar, evaporated milk, corn syrup, and butter and bring to a boil over medium heat, stirring to dissolve sugar. Boil approximately 5 minutes until mixture thickens.

2. Transfer the fondue mixture to the fondue pot and set over the heat source. Keep the fondue warm on low heat. Serve with marshmallows, fruit, and/or popcorn for dipping.

Key Lime Pie Fondue

Serves 2

This mixture can also be chilled and served as a cold fondue, making it the perfect make-ahead party or potluck dessert. If you don't have graham crackers (the traditional key lime crust), some snickerdoodle or shortbread cookies would also be great dipped in this.

Ingredients

½ cup sweetened condensed milk

½ cup key lime juice

½ cup heavy cream

½ teaspoon vanilla extract

Graham crackers

1. In a medium heavy saucepan over low heat, combine condensed milk and key lime juice. Heat, whisking constantly, until mixture is bubbly.

2. Slowly whisk in cream and vanilla.

3. Pour into a fondue pot and set over heat source on lowest setting.

4. Enjoy with graham crackers for dipping.

French Crème Fraîche Fondue

Serves 2

This is a fondue that takes a bit of prep work, so plan ahead to make this dessert. The crème fraîche needs to be prepared the day before you want to serve the fondue.

Ingredients

½ cup heavy cream

1 tablespoon buttermilk

2 medium apples, cored and cut into wedges

2 teaspoons lemon juice

8 ounces semisweet chocolate

2 tablespoons coffee liqueur

Biscotti

1. The day before you plan to serve the fondue, make the crème fraîche. In a small bowl, combine heavy cream and buttermilk, cover, and let sit in the refrigerator 24 hours.

2. Lightly brush apple wedges with lemon juice and refrigerate until ready to serve.

3. In a medium metal bowl, combine semisweet chocolate and the crème fraîche and place the bowl on top of a saucepan half filled with simmering water. Melt chocolate on low heat, stirring frequently and making sure that it doesn't boil. Stir in coffee liqueur.

4. Transfer the fondue mixture to the fondue pot and set over the heat source. Keep warm on low heat. Serve with biscotti and apple wedges for dipping.

Chocolate Honey Fondue

Serves 2

In this recipe, unsweetened chocolate balances the extra sugar in the condensed milk. For extra flavor, serve with crushed peanuts for dipping the chocolate-coated banana slices. You can find honey liqueur in most liquor stores, or you can make your own by simmering honey and water over medium heat until combined, then cooling and mixing with vodka.

Ingredients

4 medium bananas

4 ounces unsweetened chocolate

2/3 cup sweetened condensed milk

2 teaspoons honey

1 tablespoon honey liqueur

1. Peel bananas and slice. Refrigerate until ready to use bananas in the fondue.

2. In a medium metal bowl, combine unsweetened chocolate, condensed milk, and honey and place the bowl on top of a saucepan half filled with simmering water. Melt chocolate over low heat, stirring frequently and making sure that it doesn't boil.

3. Remove from the heat and stir in honey liqueur.

4. Transfer the fondue mixture to the fondue pot and set over the heat source. Keep warm over low heat. Serve with banana slices for dipping.

> **Which Fondue Pot to Use?**
> *When it comes to creating a romantic atmosphere to enjoy chocolate fondue by, nothing beats dessert fondue pots. Made of ceramic and with a single candle for the heat source, most will conveniently hold up to 2 cups of chocolate fondue.*

Peanut Butter Fondue

Serves 6

You'll want to use chunky peanut butter in this fondue, not smooth, because it adds texture and flavor to this easy-to-make fondue. And when the peanut butter and chocolate combine and melt together, it's perfection!

Ingredients

1 cup chunky natural
  peanut butter

1 cup whole milk

4 ounces milk chocolate,
  broken into pieces

4 large bananas, peeled
  and sliced

Peanut butter cookies

1. In a medium metal bowl, combine peanut butter, milk, and milk chocolate and place bowl on top of a saucepan half filled with simmering water. Melt chocolate over low to medium-low heat, stirring constantly. Make sure that it doesn't boil.

2. Transfer the fondue mixture to the fondue pot and set over the heat source. Keep the fondue warm over low heat. Serve with bananas and cookies for dipping.

Mascarpone with Baked Pears

Serves 2

The firm texture of baked pears makes an interesting contrast to the creamy mascarpone. Serve this dish with hot spiced rum for a romantic dessert for two.

Ingredients

4 firm ripe medium pears, cored and cut into chunks

¾ cup apple juice

8 ounces mascarpone cheese

¼ cup corn syrup

⅛ teaspoon ground nutmeg

¼ teaspoon ground cinnamon

3 teaspoons rum

1. Preheat oven to 350°F.

2. Place pears in a 9" × 9" shallow glass dish and pour apple juice over. Bake 30 minutes.

3. In a medium metal bowl, combine mascarpone and corn syrup and place the bowl on top of a saucepan half filled with simmering water. Melt mixture over low to medium-low heat, stirring frequently and making sure that it doesn't boil.

4. When mascarpone has melted and the fondue has the texture of custard, stir in nutmeg, cinnamon, and rum.

5. Transfer the fondue mixture to a dessert fondue pot and keep warm over low heat. Use dipping forks to spear baked pear chunks and dip into the fondue.

Peppermint Fondue

Serves 2

If you are feeling festive, crush up some candy canes to sprinkle on top of this finished fondue for a lovely presentation. This fondue tastes excellent with fresh strawberries and sliced kiwifruit for dippers, or if you are feeling a little decadent, try some chocolate cookies, shortbread cookies, marshmallows, or pretzels. If you really like peppermint flavor, you can add more peppermint liqueur to this recipe.

Ingredients

4 ounces semisweet chocolate

½ cup peppermint-flavored baking chips

3 tablespoons sour cream

6 teaspoons evaporated milk

1 tablespoon butter

1 tablespoon peppermint liqueur

1. In a medium metal bowl, combine semisweet chocolate, peppermint baking chips, sour cream, and evaporated milk and place bowl on top of a saucepan half filled with simmering water.

2. Melt chocolate over low to medium-low heat, stirring frequently and making sure that it doesn't boil. Add butter and allow to melt. Stir in peppermint liqueur.

3. Transfer the fondue mixture to the fondue pot and set over the heat source. Keep the fondue warm over low heat. Serve.

Warm Berry Compote Fondue

Serves 6

If fresh berries aren't in season, don't hesitate to use frozen ones in this dish. This compote is delicious served with croissants and biscuits for dipping. It can also be ladled over ice cream as a topping or used as a sauce for sponge cakes and pound cakes. Just add whipped cream.

Ingredients

1 cup pitted cherries

1 cup blueberries

1 cup blackberries

1 cup raspberries

1½ cups sugar

½ cup water

1 tablespoon cornstarch

2 tablespoons Grand Marnier

Croissants

Biscuits

1. In a medium heavy saucepan over medium heat, combine berries, sugar, and water. Cook, stirring often until sugar is dissolved and mixture is beginning to bubble. Reduce heat slightly and simmer 15 minutes.

2. In a small bowl, dissolve cornstarch in Grand Marnier. Increase heat under berries and bring to a boil. Add cornstarch mixture and cook, stirring constantly until mixture is thickened.

3. Pour berries into one or more fondue pots and place over heat source over low heat. Serve with croissants and biscuits for dipping.

My Favorite Things Fondue

Serves 8

Kids and kids at heart will equally love this dish—with sprinkles, doughnuts, and candy, who wouldn't love it? This dish is perfect for a casual party with friends. You can put out everyone's favorite cookies and candies and get to dipping!

Ingredients

1½ pounds milk chocolate

1 cup heavy cream

2 cups flaked coconut

2 cups multicolored sprinkles

Chocolate sandwich cookies

Crispy rice treat bites

Doughnut holes

Large marshmallows

1. In a medium saucepan over low heat, combine chocolate and cream. Warm, stirring constantly, until chocolate is melted and mixture is creamy.

2. Divide coconut into eight dipping bowls and do the same with sprinkles.

3. Pour chocolate mixture into one or more fondue pots and place over heat source on lowest setting.

4. Allow guests to dip cookies, rice treats, doughnuts, and marshmallows in chocolate, then roll dippers in coconut or sprinkles.

Kid-Safe Fondue

Chocolate stays melted for a good while. If you're hosting a party of very small children, consider dividing the chocolate fondue among several microwave-safe bowls. You'll eliminate the stress of having an open flame on the table. Let them dunk away, and if the chocolate starts to stiffen, just pop it in the microwave for a few seconds.

Bittersweet Chocolate Orange Fondue

Serves 6

Grand Marnier is an orange-flavored liqueur, and when combined with the orange zest they create a heavenly citrus scent in this bittersweet chocolate fondue. This dish is reminiscent of those orange-shaped chocolate candies that you smash to open. The almonds add a satisfying crunch and a nice presentation to the top.

Ingredients

1 pound bittersweet chocolate

⅔ cup heavy cream

2 tablespoons orange zest

¼ cup Grand Marnier liqueur

1 cup slivered almonds

Stemmed strawberries

Shortbread cookies

1. In a medium saucepan over low heat, combine chocolate and cream. Warm, stirring constantly, until chocolate is melted and mixture is smooth.

2. Stir in orange zest and Grand Marnier.

3. Pour chocolate mixture into one or more fondue pots and place over heat source on lowest setting.

4. Sprinkle almonds over the top for garnish. Serve with strawberries and shortbread cookies for dipping.

> **Getting Zesty**
>
> *Citrus zest is the colored, outer part of the fruit peel. The white pith, just beneath the zest, is bitter and should not be added to dessert recipes.*

Louisiana Butter Pecan Fondue

Serves 6

Think of this as pecan pie in fondue form! Nuts like pecans are high in healthy fats. That makes them good for you, but also makes them perishable. Store nuts in airtight bags in the freezer to keep flavor. Serve this nutty fondue with shortbread cookies, vanilla wafers, or biscotti for dippers.

Ingredients

2 cups pecan halves

½ cup butter

1 cup packed brown sugar

½ cup corn syrup

2 cups heavy cream

1 teaspoon vanilla extract

Shortbread cookies

1. In a heavy Dutch oven, combine pecans with butter. Cook over medium heat, stirring frequently, until pecans are toasted.

2. Stir in brown sugar and corn syrup. Cook until sugar is melted and mixture is bubbly. Add cream and bring to a boil. Reduce heat and simmer 2 minutes. Add vanilla.

3. Pour pecan mixture into one or more fondue pots. Set over heat source on low heat and serve with shortbread cookies for dipping.

Chocolate Peanut Butter Fondue

Serves 6

This fondue uses both peanut butter and peanuts to create the rich peanut flavor in this age-old flavor mash-up. For variety, you could consider switching the peanut butter with cashew butter or almond butter.

Ingredients

1 pound milk chocolate

1 cup creamy natural peanut butter

1 tablespoon butter

1 cup heavy cream

1 cup chopped peanuts

Pretzel rods

Fingerling bananas

1. In a medium saucepan over low heat, combine chocolate, peanut butter, butter, and cream. Heat, stirring constantly, until chocolate is melted and mixture is smooth.

2. Pour chocolate peanut butter mixture into one or more fondue pots and place over heat source on lowest setting.

3. Sprinkle peanuts over the top of the fondue. Serve with pretzels and bananas for dipping.

> ### Peanut Butter au Naturel
> *It's best to use a natural peanut butter in most recipes. Commercial brands have emulsifiers that may affect melting ability. Be sure to stir natural nut butters well to blend oils that may have separated.*

Crème Anglaise Fondue

Serves 6

This fondue is so creamy and delicious you'll have to stop your guests from taking out a spoon and slurping this luscious cream. It tastes delicious on fresh fruit, but if you are feeling especially decadent, break out the chocolate cake and get to dipping!

Ingredients

6 large egg yolks

½ cup sugar

2 cups heavy cream

1 cup whole milk

1 teaspoon vanilla extract

2 tablespoons Irish cream liqueur

Quartered fresh peaches

Stemmed whole strawberries

1. In a large bowl, whisk together egg yolks and sugar until they're light yellow and thick.

2. Pour cream and milk into a medium saucepan and cook over medium heat until just scalded. Slowly pour hot cream mixture into egg mixture, whisking constantly to keep cream from cooking eggs.

3. Pour eggs and cream back into saucepan and cook over medium heat, stirring constantly until mixture is thick enough to coat a spoon. Stir in vanilla and liqueur.

4. Pour sauce into one or more fondue pots and place over heat source set to low heat. Serve with peaches and strawberries for dipping.

Coconut Milk and Macadamia Nut Fondue

Serves 6

The blend of coconut and macadamia nuts in this fondue is a tropical treat. Serve this with chocolate pound cake cubes and pineapple spears or maybe try some grapes and mandarin oranges to add some color and pop.

Ingredients

1 cup sweetened condensed milk

2 cups coconut milk

½ teaspoon coconut extract

1 tablespoon macadamia nut butter

2 tablespoons macadamia nut liqueur

2 cups chopped macadamia nuts

2 cups shredded coconut

Pineapple spears

Chocolate pound cake cubes

1. To a blender, add condensed milk, coconut milk, coconut extract, and macadamia nut butter. Blend until smooth. Pour into a medium saucepan over low heat and heat until mixture is bubbling.

2. Add liqueur and stir well. Remove from heat and pour mixture into one or more fondue pots. Set over heat source on low heat.

3. Divide nuts and coconut into individual dipping dishes. Encourage guests to dip pineapple and pound cake cubes in fondue, then coat them with nuts or coconut.

> ### Do-It-Yourself Nut Butter
> *Specialty shops carry a range of nut butters. To make your own, simply pour a cup of macadamia nuts into a food processor with a metal blade. Drizzle a few drops of almond oil into the bowl and pulse until nuts are creamy. Add salt if desired.*

Mascarpone and Calvados Fondue

Serves 6

Mascarpone, a creamy fresh cheese, stars in the famous Italian dessert tiramisu. But it's also very tasty in other desserts like this fondue! Calvados is an apple or pear brandy that is the perfect complement to this velvety cheese.

Ingredients

2 cups mascarpone cheese

½ cup heavy cream

¼ cup Calvados

1 teaspoon vanilla extract

¼ teaspoon ground nutmeg

Tart and sweet apple slices

1. In a medium saucepan over medium heat, combine mascarpone and cream. Cook, stirring constantly, until cheese is melted and mixture is bubbly.

2. Stir in Calvados, vanilla, and nutmeg. Remove from heat.

3. Pour into one or more fondue pots and place over heat source on low heat.

4. Serve with apple slices for dipping.

> ### Eau de Vie
> *Dozens of different varieties of apples go into the production of Calvados, an oak barrel—aged brandy that originated in the Normandy region of France. Other clear fruit brandies, such as pear or plum, can be added to dessert sauces or even cheese fondue.*

Chocolate Banana Fondue

Serves 4

Milk chocolate or Toblerone can be substituted for the semisweet chocolate chips. Use four (100-gram) milk chocolate Toblerone bars and adjust the cream as necessary. The banana chutney you'll create for this fondue is also amazing over vanilla ice cream, so make a double batch! Serve this fondue with sliced apples, sliced bananas, and plain biscuits for dipping.

Sweet Banana Chutney Ingredients

2 large bananas, peeled and thinly sliced

⅓ cup balsamic vinegar

1 teaspoon brown sugar

¼ teaspoon allspice

1 teaspoon water

Fondue Ingredients

½ cup half and half

1½ cups semisweet chocolate chips

⅓ cup Sweet Banana Chutney

¼ cup crushed peanuts

1. **For chutney:** In a medium saucepan, bring sliced bananas and balsamic vinegar to a boil over medium-high heat. Continue to cook mixture, stirring frequently, until bananas and vinegar are fully blended.

2. Stir in brown sugar and allspice. Add water and heat the mixture through. Remove from heat and allow to cool. Store in the refrigerator until needed.

3. **For fondue:** In a medium metal bowl, combine half and half and semisweet chocolate and place bowl over a saucepan half filled with simmering water. Melt chocolate over low to medium-low heat, stirring continuously and making sure it doesn't boil. When chocolate is melted, stir in ⅓ cup Sweet Banana Chutney, saving the remainder for another time.

4. Garnish the fondue with crushed peanuts. Keep the fondue warm over low heat while serving.

Bourbon and Butterscotch Fondue

Serves 6

The toasty brown sugar flavor of bourbon pairs nicely with the butterscotch in this fondue. You can make this fondue without the alcohol; just increase the amount of cream and add a teaspoon of vanilla or rum extract. Serve this fondue with slices of green apples, pound cake cubes, or shortbread cookies.

Ingredients

2 cups sugar

⅔ cup water

1 tablespoon lemon juice

½ cup butter

1 cup heavy cream

¼ cup bourbon

Pound cake cubes

1. In a large heavy saucepan, combine sugar, water, and lemon juice. Cook over medium heat, stirring until sugar has dissolved. Increase heat to medium-high and cook, stirring often until mixture is golden.

2. Remove pan from heat and carefully add butter. Stir in cream a little at a time. When cream is thoroughly blended, allow mixture to cool slightly. When fondue is no longer bubbling, stir in bourbon.

3. Transfer butterscotch mixture to one or more fondue pots and place over heat source set to low heat. Serve with pound cake cubes for dipping.

Spirited Fondue

High-proof alcohol can be added to cheese and dessert fondues in small amounts. However, you should never substitute spirits for wine in a Bacchus fondue. At high temperatures, whiskey and other spirits are inflammable.

Marshmallow Fondue

Serves 6

This fondue is alive with the flavors of caramel, chocolate, and peppermint—and of course marshmallow! To transform this into an adult dessert fondue, simply add 2 tablespoons of either kirsch or peppermint liqueur.

Ingredients

½ cup evaporated milk

10 caramel candies

1⅓ cups semisweet chocolate chips

1 cup peppermint chips

60–80 miniature marshmallows

1. In a medium metal bowl, combine evaporated milk and caramels and place bowl on top of a saucepan half filled with simmering water. When caramels are approximately half melted, add chocolate and peppermint chips. Melt over low to medium-low heat, stirring frequently and making sure the chocolate doesn't boil.

2. Transfer the fondue mixture to the fondue pot and set over the heat source. Keep the fondue warm over low heat.

3. Take two miniature marshmallows and stick one on each prong of the dipping fork. Draw through the chocolate and enjoy.

Chocolate Mint Fondue

Serves 6

Luscious and creamy mint chocolate with chocolate wafers dipped in, this fondue is a delicious treat. If you can't find (or don't want to buy) crème de menthe for this fondue, just look for mint-flavored chocolate bars. Melt the bars with cream and you can skip the crème de menthe.

Ingredients

1 pound semisweet chocolate

⅔ cup heavy cream

½ teaspoon peppermint extract

¼ cup crème de menthe

Chocolate wafers

1. In a medium saucepan over low heat, combine chocolate and cream. Heat, stirring constantly, until chocolate is melted and mixture is smooth.

2. Stir in peppermint extract and crème de menthe.

3. Pour chocolate mixture into the fondue pot and place over heat source on lowest setting. Serve with chocolate wafers for dipping.

Harvest Apple Fondue

Serves 6

Chocolate and cinnamon make a perfect coating for your apples, and the peanuts give it that extra nutty crunch. Sweet Spartan apples work very well in this recipe. Serve this fondue with the red apple wedges or try cider doughnut chunks, small chocolate chip cookies, or graham crackers.

Ingredients

1½ cups peanuts

4 large red apples, cored and cut into wedges

½ cup whipping cream

¾ cup semisweet chocolate chips

½ cup cinnamon baking chips

2 teaspoons sugar

1. Crush peanuts in a blender or food processor. Place apple wedges in the refrigerator to chill.

2. In a medium metal bowl, combine cream and both kinds of chips and place bowl over a saucepan half filled with simmering water. Melt mixture over low to medium-low heat, stirring continuously and making sure mixture doesn't boil. Stir in sugar.

3. Transfer mixture to a fondue pot and set over the heat source over low heat.

4. Remove apple from the refrigerator and set on the table. Set out individual bowls of crushed peanuts for each person. Have guests dip apple slices in the fondue and then roll in the crushed peanuts.

> **Using Fruit in Chocolate Fondue**
> *It tastes great, but fruit dipped in warm chocolate can be a little messy to eat. To keep the chocolate from dripping off, refrigerate the sliced fruit until the fondue is ready to serve. The chocolate cools down when it meets the chilled fruit, making it harden slightly.*

Chocolate Marshmallow Fondue

Serves 6

While graham crackers are a perfect dipper for this fondue, it is also delicious with fresh strawberries. Sprinkle a few unmelted marshmallows over the top of this fondue for a fun and delicious garnish.

Ingredients

1 pound semisweet chocolate

1 cup heavy cream

2 cups miniature marshmallows

1 teaspoon vanilla extract

2 tablespoons vanilla liqueur

Graham cracker sticks

1. In a medium saucepan over low heat, combine chocolate and cream. Heat, stirring constantly, until chocolate is melted and mixture is smooth.

2. Stir in marshmallows, vanilla, and liqueur. Mix until blended.

3. Pour chocolate mixture into one or more fondue pots and place over heat source on lowest setting. Serve with graham cracker sticks for dipping.

Chocolate Bar Fondue

Serves 4

The caramel flavor in Mars bars combines nicely with tart apple dippers in this fondue. For a more adult version, add 1 tablespoon Kahlúa or kirsch to the melted chocolate before serving.

Ingredients

6 large apples

4 regular-sized Mars bars

½ cup whipping cream

1. Cut apples into six slices each. Refrigerate until ready to use in the fondue.

2. Unwrap chocolate bars and cut into several pieces. Combine a few pieces of chocolate with whipping cream in a medium metal bowl and place on top of a saucepan half filled with simmering water.

3. Stir frequently over low heat, making sure mixture doesn't come to a boil. Continue adding more chocolate, a few pieces at a time, until all chocolate is melted.

4. Transfer mixture to the fondue pot and set over the heat source. Keep the fondue warm over low heat. Serve with apple slices for dipping.

Turn Your Favorite Chocolate Bar Into a Fondue

It's easy! Just break the chocolate bar into several pieces, combine with cream, and melt in a metal bowl placed over a saucepan half filled with barely simmering water. Start with a small amount of cream and add more if needed. (It takes about 2 tablespoons to melt each chocolate bar, depending on the exact size of the bar and the specific ingredients.) Be sure not to let the chocolate boil. For best results, stick with one or possibly two chocolate bar brands.

Crème Caramel Fondue

Serves 2

This fondue tastes like your favorite caramel candies except warm and gooey and perfect for dipping fruit in. If you wish, you can make this fondue nonalcoholic by omitting the brandy and adding $\frac{1}{2}$ teaspoon vanilla extract instead. This fondue is perfect with dippers like apples, apricots, and bananas, or you can also try wafer cookies or ladyfingers too.

Ingredients

½ cup heavy cream

10 caramel candies

1 tablespoon brandy

1 tablespoon brown sugar

Apple slices

Dried apricots

Banana slices

1. In a medium heavy saucepan over medium-low heat, combine cream and caramels. Cook and stir until caramels are melted and mixture is bubbly. Add brandy.

2. Pour mixture into a fondue pot and place over heat source on low heat. Sprinkle brown sugar on top.

3. Enjoy with apples, apricots, and bananas for dipping.

Spiced Apple Fondue

Serves 6

To prevent discoloration and add extra flavor, lightly coat the apple wedges in pineapple or lemon juice and refrigerate until ready to use in the fondue. The apple schnapps gives the fondue that extra shot of apple flavor that really makes this dish a standout.

Ingredients

¼ cup half and half

1¾ cups semisweet chocolate chips

½ teaspoon ground cinnamon

2 tablespoons apple schnapps

3 medium Spartan apples, cored and cut into wedges

1. In a medium metal bowl, combine half and half and chocolate and place bowl over a saucepan half filled with simmering water. Melt chips over low to medium-low heat, stirring continuously and making sure mixture doesn't boil.

2. When chocolate is melted, transfer mixture to the fondue pot and set over the heat source. Stir in cinnamon and apple schnapps. Keep the fondue warm over low heat. Serve with apple wedges for dipping.

Yin-Yang Fondue

Serves 6

Like the yin-yang symbol of balance, this fondue captures the flavors of both white and milk chocolate to create a mouthwatering treat. White chocolate has a subtle flavor that comes from the addition of vanilla extract and other ingredients into the cocoa butter. Serve this with slices of green and red apples and cantaloupe chunks for dippers.

Ingredients

8 ounces white chocolate, broken into pieces

8 ounces semisweet chocolate, broken into pieces

½ cup evaporated milk

½ teaspoon ground cinnamon

¼ cup kirsch

6 cups mixed apple and cantaloupe slices

1. In a medium metal bowl, combine white chocolate, semisweet chocolate, and evaporated milk and then place the bowl on top of a saucepan half filled with simmering water. Melt mixture on low to medium-low heat, making sure that it doesn't boil.

2. When chocolate has melted, stir in cinnamon and kirsch.

3. Transfer the fondue mixture to the fondue pot and set over the heat source. Keep the fondue warm on low heat. Serve with apple and cantaloupe slices for dipping.

Tiramisu with Cream Fondue

Serves 4

This fondue will give you all the flavors of the classic Italian dessert without all the intensive prep—soaking ladyfingers, no thanks! The ladyfingers become the dippers in the fondue version of this dessert. Feel free to substitute a good Marsala wine for the rum.

Ingredients

1 pound mascarpone cheese

¼ cup light cream

¼ cup confectioners' sugar

¼ cup strong, fresh-brewed espresso coffee, divided

1 tablespoon plus 1 teaspoon powdered hot chocolate

2 teaspoons cornstarch

2 tablespoons rum

4 large egg yolks

2 teaspoons ground cinnamon

24 ladyfingers

1. In a medium metal bowl, combine mascarpone, light cream, confectioners' sugar, and 4 teaspoons espresso and place bowl on top of a saucepan half filled with simmering water. Melt mixture over low to medium-low heat, stirring frequently and making sure that it doesn't boil.

2. When mascarpone has melted and has a texture close to pudding, stir in hot chocolate.

3. In a small bowl, dissolve cornstarch in rum. Stir mixture into the fondue.

4. Whisk in egg yolks to thicken.

5. Transfer the fondue mixture to the fondue pot and set over the heat source. Keep warm over low heat. Just before serving, sprinkle with cinnamon.

6. Brush ladyfingers with remaining espresso and serve with the fondue for dipping.

Doughnut Fondue

Serves 6

This is the perfect fondue dip for doughnuts. Rich, chocolaty, and creamy, this tasty treat may cause you to never buy a frosted doughnut at a store again. Not a fan of doughnuts (if that could even be possible!)? This fondue also tastes delicious served with fresh cantaloupe slices for dipping.

Ingredients

8 ounces semisweet chocolate, broken into pieces

1 cup cinnamon baking chips

6 tablespoons sour cream

6 tablespoons evaporated milk

¼ cup half and half

2 tablespoons butter

¼ teaspoon ground allspice

Plain doughnuts

1. In a medium metal bowl, combine chocolate, baking chips, sour cream, evaporated milk, and half and half and place bowl on top of a saucepan half filled with simmering water. Melt mixture over low to medium-low heat, making sure that it doesn't boil.

2. Add butter and allow to melt. Stir in allspice.

3. Transfer the fondue mixture to a fondue pot and set over the heat source. Keep the fondue warm over low heat.

4. Serve with doughnuts for dipping. Doughnuts can be eaten whole or cut into pieces and speared with a dipping fork.

Sweet-and-Sour Tropical Fondue

Serves 6

Enjoy the flavors of the tropics right on your table! For an added touch, try rolling the dipped banana slices in grated coconut before eating. If you can't find a tropical fruit mix, you can use any dried fruit mix you like.

Ingredients

¾ cup sour cream

2 tablespoons butter

2 cups chocolate macaroons

2 tablespoons Kahlúa

4 medium bananas, peeled and sliced

2 cups tropical dried fruit mix

1. In a medium metal bowl, combine sour cream, butter, and chocolate macaroons and place the bowl over a saucepan half filled with simmering water. Heat mixture over medium-low heat, stirring constantly. Do not let mixture boil.

2. When chocolate is melted, stir in Kahlúa. Transfer mixture to the fondue pot and set over the heat source. Keep the fondue warm over low heat.

3. Serve with bananas and dried fruit for dipping.

Mexican Chocolate Fondue with Kahlúa and Strawberries

Serves 6

The cinnamon, nutmeg, and cloves in this fondue elevate it above the standard chocolate fondue and give it a spicy earthiness. For a different flavor, try substituting half the semisweet chocolate with unsweetened chocolate and adding honey to your liking. Serve this with the suggested strawberries or mix it up with some kiwi slices, orange pieces, bite-sized brownies, or doughnut hole treats!

Ingredients

12 ounces semisweet chocolate, broken into pieces

½ cup half and half

¾ cup evaporated milk

1 teaspoon ground cinnamon

½ teaspoon ground nutmeg

¼ teaspoon ground cloves

1 tablespoon Kahlúa

1 pound fresh strawberries, hulled

1. In a medium metal bowl, combine chocolate, half and half, and evaporated milk and place bowl on top of a saucepan half filled with simmering water. Melt mixture over low to medium-low heat, making sure that it doesn't boil.

2. When chocolate is melted, stir in cinnamon, nutmeg, and cloves. Stir in Kahlúa.

3. Transfer the fondue mixture to the fondue pot and set over the heat source. Keep the fondue warm over low heat.

4. Serve with strawberries for dipping.

> **Burned Chocolate Cure**
> *Burning chocolate causes the skin to seize and tighten until the texture resembles pudding. To reliquefy burned chocolate, stir 1 or 2 tablespoons butter into the chocolate mixture.*

Caramel Popcorn Fondue

Serves 6

This fondue tastes like the salty and sweet caramel corn you'd get at a carnival or fair. For best results, prepare the popcorn on the same day you are making the fondue. You could also use it with pieces of rice cakes in a pinch.

Popcorn Ingredients

6 cups Popcorn Twists

6 tablespoons corn syrup

4 tablespoons butter

8 teaspoons brown sugar

½ teaspoon ground cinnamon

½ teaspoon ground nutmeg

Creamy Caramel Fondue Ingredients

2 cups white sugar

1 cup evaporated milk

4 tablespoons corn syrup

4 tablespoons butter

1. **For popcorn:** Preheat the oven to 250°F. Grease a baking tray.

2. Lay Popcorn Twists out flat on the tray.

3. In a small saucepan, melt corn syrup, butter, and brown sugar over medium-low heat. Stir in cinnamon and nutmeg. Pour over popcorn. Bake 30 minutes. Cool.

4. **For fondue:** In a medium saucepan over medium heat, combine sugar, evaporated milk, corn syrup, and butter and bring to a boil stirring to dissolve sugar. Boil approximately 5 minutes until mixture thickens.

5. Transfer the fondue mixture to the fondue pot and set over the heat source. Keep the fondue warm over low heat.

6. Use the Popcorn Twists as dippers with the caramel fondue.

Honey Almond Fondue Flambé

Serves 2

This fondue comes with some added flair—you set it on fire! Using cognac lighted on a spoon to ignite the remaining cognac prevents you from having to lean over to light the fondue, which could be dangerous.

Ingredients

4 (3.5-ounce) Toblerone honey and almond milk chocolate bars, broken into pieces

½ cup half and half

2 tablespoons cognac

Banana and pear slices

1. In a medium metal bowl, combine chocolate and half and half and place the bowl over a saucepan half filled with boiling water. When chocolate is melted, transfer the fondue mixture to the fondue pot and set on the heat source.

2. Reserve 1 teaspoon cognac and add remainder on top of the fondue. Fill a dessert spoon with the 1 teaspoon cognac. Light cognac on the spoon. Use lighted cognac to light brandy on chocolate. Once cognac has burned out, the fondue is ready to eat.

3. Keep the fondue warm over low heat. Serve with banana and pear slices for dipping.

Toblerone—The Original Chocolate Fondue

Switzerland is famous as the birthplace of cheese fondue, but fewer people realize that a famous Swiss chocolate bar inspired the creation of chocolate-based dessert fondues. The original chocolate dessert fondue was made with Swiss Toblerone, an oversized chocolate bar loaded with honey and almonds. Today, many people still feel Toblerone is the best choice for a chocolate fondue.

Cherry Mascarpone Fondue

Serves 6

Mascarpone is the ultimate dessert cheese, with the texture of a soft, silky cream cheese and slightly tart, clean flavor. It pairs perfectly with the tartness of cherries. Serve this fondue with strawberries, apples, cherries, shortbread cookies, biscotti, and ladyfingers.

Ingredients

1 pound mascarpone cheese

¼ cup kirsch

1 tablespoon cornstarch

3 tablespoons confectioners' sugar

3 large eggs

1 cup chopped and pitted cherries

1. In a medium metal bowl, whisk together cheese, kirsch, cornstarch, and confectioners' sugar and place bowl on top of a saucepan half filled with simmering water. Melt mixture over low to medium-low heat, making sure that it doesn't boil.

2. In a medium mixing bowl, whip eggs on medium speed until they're light and frothy.

3. When cheese is melted and mixture is hot, slowly pour a ladle of hot cheese into eggs while beating eggs. Pour eggs into the double boiler and whisk together briskly. Stir in cherries.

4. Pour mixture into one or more fondue pots and place over heat source on low heat.

Temper, Temper

Eggs must be warmed slightly and quickly before being whisked into hot liquid. Otherwise, you'll have bits of hard, cooked egg in your mixture. It takes practice, but the trick is to add hot liquid slowly while keeping the eggs moving.

White Peach Shortcake Fondue

Serves 6

White peaches, in addition to having a lighter flesh than their yellow cousins, also have a sweeter flavor that is lower in acid, so they are perfect for desserts. For this shortcake you'll be using the traditional southern favorite: sweet biscuits. If you don't have any shortening, you can substitute butter.

Sweet Shortcake Biscuits Ingredients

3 cups all-purpose flour

⅓ cup sugar

4 teaspoons baking powder

½ teaspoon salt

¾ cup shortening, chilled

1 teaspoon almond extract

1½ cups heavy cream

Fondue Ingredients

4 cups Crème Anglaise Fondue (see recipe in this part), chilled

6 cups sliced white peaches

6 cups lightly sweetened whipped cream

1. Preheat oven to 400°F.

2. **For biscuits:** In a large bowl, combine flour, sugar, baking powder, and salt. Whisk to blend and remove any clumps.

3. Add shortening and cut in with two knives or a pastry blender until mixture resembles coarse meal.

4. In a small bowl, add almond extract to cream and then stir into flour mixture. Use moistened fingers to blend dough and work it into a ball. Cover and refrigerate until chilled.

5. Press dough into a 1"-thick square. With a small biscuit cutter, cut twelve circles. Place on a greased cookie sheet. Bake until nicely browned, about 15 minutes. Allow to cool.

6. **For fondue:** Pour chilled Crème Anglaise into one or two serving bowls. Place a shallow bowl or glass pie plate of fresh peach slices next to each bowl.

7. Divide whipped cream into dipping bowls for each guest.

8. Split warm biscuits and place on serving platters. Encourage guests to dip peaches in Crème Anglaise, dip in whipped cream, and enjoy with bites of warm biscuits.

The Rose of Fruits

Peaches are members of the rose family, which may explain their wonderful fragrance. These floral notes make white peaches perfect for dishes like fruit salad or just for eating fresh off the tree! White peaches have less acidity than yellow peaches, taste sweeter than their more colorful cousins, and tend to be more delicate as they can bruise more easily.

Butter Maple Raisin Sauce

Serves 6

This fondue is perfect for dipping French toast sticks or bits of pancakes or waffles in. That's right; it's fondue for breakfast or dessert! Kids absolutely love this fondue. Serve it on winter morning for the ultimate comfort food hit!

Ingredients

½ cup butter

1 teaspoon ground cinnamon

1½ cups raisins

2 cups maple syrup

¼ cup water

French toast sticks

Waffle pieces

1. In a medium saucepan over medium heat, combine butter and cinnamon. Stir until butter is melted and cinnamon is blended. Add raisins, syrup, and water. Bring to a boil, then remove from heat.

2. Pour maple sauce into one or more fondue pots. Place over heat source over low heat and serve with French toast and waffle pieces for dipping.

> ### Sap Lovers
> *Authentic maple syrup—the kind distilled from maple tree sap—is a gourmet gift from nature. It's considerably more expensive than maple-flavored corn syrup but worth the price. You'll appreciate the complex flavors in fondues and other dishes.*

Colorful Candy Fondue

Serves 8

This is a traditional fondue that you take to the next level with colorful candies and treats. This fondue is a big hit with the younger crowd, but anyone will enjoy this fun and colorful fondue!

Ingredients

1½ pounds milk chocolate

1 cup heavy cream

4 cups Skittles, miniature M&M's, or Reese's Pieces

Large marshmallows

24–32 miniature cupcakes, unfrosted

Large pretzel sticks

1. In a medium saucepan over low heat, combine chocolate and cream. Warm, stirring constantly, until chocolate is melted and mixture is smooth.

2. Divide candies over eight dipping bowls.

3. Pour chocolate mixture into one or more fondue pots and place over heat source on low heat. Place marshmallows, cupcakes, and pretzels on serving platters. Allow guests to coat dippers with fondue and roll in candies to coat.

Chocolate Cherry Cordial Fondue

Serves 6

This fondue tastes like the cherry cordial candies you see every holiday but in a creamier form. Cherry-infused cream gives this fondue a rich cherry flavor that is complemented by the kirsch.

Ingredients

1 cup heavy cream

1 cup fresh or frozen sweet cherries, pitted

1 pound semisweet chocolate, chopped

2 tablespoons kirsch

Stemmed cherries

Biscotti

1. In a blender, combine cream and cherries. Pulse until mixture is blended and cherries are puréed. Strain cherry-flavored cream into a medium saucepan and heat over low heat until just bubbling.

2. Reduce heat and add chopped chocolate. Stir constantly until chocolate is melted and mixture is smooth. Add kirsch and stir.

3. Pour chocolate mixture into one or more fondue pots and place over heat source on lowest setting. Serve with stemmed cherries and biscotti for dipping.

A Bowl of Cherries

Most fresh cherries on the market are sweet cherries. Tart cherries turn up in jams and jellies and occasionally as frozen cherries. Maraschino cherries aren't a type of cherry at all. They're sweet cherries that have been soaked in sugar syrup, flavored with a touch of almond, and dyed red.

Homemade Butterscotch Fondue

Serves 6

The warm, rich flavor of butterscotch presented here is a delicious fondue perfect for dipping your favorite cakes and pastries in. Stirring the mixture continuously once the butter and whipping cream are added keeps it from hardening into butterscotch candy.

Ingredients

2 cups sugar

½ cup water

4 tablespoons butter

½ cup whipping cream

2 tablespoons corn syrup

½ cup chopped unsalted peanuts

Marshmallows, fruit, or cake

1. In a medium saucepan over medium heat, combine sugar and water and cook, stirring to dissolve sugar. When sugar is dissolved, turn up the heat and boil mixture at least 5 minutes until sugar turns a golden color.

2. If sugar has formed clumps, leave on medium heat and stir to melt the clumps. Once the sugar is evenly dissolved, remove from the heat and immediately stir in butter and whipping cream. Stir vigorously to keep mixture from hardening.

3. Stir in corn syrup and chopped peanuts. Serve unheated in a bowl with marshmallows, fruit, or cake for dipping.

US/Metric Conversion Chart

Volume Conversions

US Volume Measure	Metric Equivalent
⅛ teaspoon	0.5 milliliter
¼ teaspoon	1 milliliter
½ teaspoon	2 milliliters
1 teaspoon	5 milliliters
½ tablespoon	7 milliliters
1 tablespoon (3 teaspoons)	15 milliliters
2 tablespoons (1 fluid ounce)	30 milliliters
¼ cup (4 tablespoons)	60 milliliters
⅓ cup	90 milliliters
½ cup (4 fluid ounces)	125 milliliters
⅔ cup	160 milliliters
¾ cup (6 fluid ounces)	180 milliliters
1 cup (16 tablespoons)	250 milliliters
1 pint (2 cups)	500 milliliters
1 quart (4 cups)	1 liter (about)

Weight Conversions

US Weight Measure	Metric Equivalent
½ ounce	15 grams
1 ounce	30 grams
2 ounces	60 grams
3 ounces	85 grams
¼ pound (4 ounces)	115 grams
½ pound (8 ounces)	225 grams
¾ pound (12 ounces)	340 grams
1 pound (16 ounces)	454 grams

Oven Temperature Conversions

Degrees Fahrenheit	Degrees Celsius
200 degrees F	95 degrees C
250 degrees F	120 degrees C
275 degrees F	135 degrees C
300 degrees F	150 degrees C
325 degrees F	160 degrees C
350 degrees F	180 degrees C
375 degrees F	190 degrees C
400 degrees F	205 degrees C
425 degrees F	220 degrees C
450 degrees F	230 degrees C

Baking Pan Sizes

American	Metric
8 x 1½ inch round baking pan	20 x 4 cm cake tin
9 x 1½ inch round baking pan	23 x 3.5 cm cake tin
11 x 7 x 1½ inch baking pan	28 x 18 x 4 cm baking tin
13 x 9 x 2 inch baking pan	30 x 20 x 5 cm baking tin
2 quart rectangular baking dish	30 x 20 x 3 cm baking tin
15 x 10 x 2 inch baking pan	30 x 25 x 2 cm baking tin (Swiss roll tin)
9 inch pie plate	22 x 4 or 23 x 4 cm pie plate
7 or 8 inch springform pan	18 or 20 cm springform or loose bottom cake tin
9 x 5 x 3 inch loaf pan	23 x 13 x 7 cm or 2 lb narrow loaf or pâté tin
1½ quart casserole	1.5 liter casserole
2 quart casserole	2 liter casserole

Index